A Journey Through America

American Government, History, Geography and Citizenship in Simplified English

Elaine Kirn

West Los Angeles College

Authors and Editors

First Edition

9 8 7 6 5 4 3 2 1

Published in The United States by Authors and Editors, P.O. Box 1396, Culver City, CA 90232-1396.

ISBN 0-9627878-2-5

Manufactured in the United States of America

Series Design and Production: Etcetera Graphics, Canoga Park, CA
Typesetting: Etcetera Graphics

Acknowledgements

Thanks to the ESL coordinators and instructors of the Los Angeles Community College District and surrounding schools for supporting this project and offering helpful suggestions.

And as usual, thanks to a hard-working staff and free-lancers:

Chuck Alessio for putting it all together,
Vicki Shipley for skillful revisions,
Joel Lewin for being everywhere,
and all of us for long, long workdays and evenings.

Contents

A Journey Through America

A Journey Through America is a book of simplified civics material directed especially toward new readers, students with reading problems, and speakers of English as a Second Language. It is appropriate for both home study and classroom use. It offers an easily-comprehensible overview of topics commonly covered in social studies and citizenship courses.

A Journey Through America is designed for individuals who have some level of proficiency in understanding and speaking the English language and who comprehend reading material of at least a fourth-grade level. If they are second-language learners who have placed into Level 3 (low-intermediate) or above of a six-level ESL program, they are likely to succeed with the materials. Students at a higher level can profit from use of *A Journey Through America* as preparation for more advanced texts.

A Journey Through America is based on curriculum outlines developed by the Los Angeles Community College District (LACCD) and the Los Angeles County Community College Consortium for Amnesty, now CCENC (Community College Educators of New Californians). These outlines were approved by the California State Department of Education and the Immigration and Naturalization Service for implementation in classes funded by State Legislative Impact Assistance Grants (SLIAG).

The information in the book is derived largely from three texts issued by the Federal government: *United States History 1600-1987, U.S. Government Structure,* and *Citizenship Education and Naturalization Information* (U.S. Department of Justice, Immigration and Naturalization Service, 1987).

The book is divided into ten numbered units, each subdivided into several lettered modules. Each module consists of four pages of material, designed for one or more class periods of instruction with follow up (homework and/or review). These can be studied or presented in any desired order.

Accompanying Materials

Accompanying *A Journey Through America* is a detailed instructor's manual. Because it offers general and specific suggestions for presentation of the ten units, it will not only streamline lesson planning for experienced teachers but can also serve as a training manual for new ones. It also provides:

- An objective test for each module of the book.

- An Answer Key for both text material and tests.

- Information of interest primarily to applicants for citizenship, in simplified English.

- A list of one hundred citizenship test questions and answers published and distributed by the INS.

- Extra modules of material on state and local geography and history, which can serve as a model for lessons about your state and city.

For classroom use, permission is granted to duplicate the materials in the instructor's manual.

English Through Citizenship: A Question and Answer Game presents an opportunity for cooperative learning and/or competition in the Civics classroom. The game can be used independently or can serve as a reinforcement for the information in the *Journey Through America* text and tests.

For additional information, contact:

Authors and Editors
P.O. Box 1396
Culver City, CA 90232-1396
Tel: (213) 836-2014

Getting Acquainted

Module 1A: Name and Address

A Names

		father's last name	mother's maiden name
NAME	Robert	William	O'Donnell-Brown
	First	Middle	Last

Barbara	Anderson	Smith
Given Name	Maiden Name (former last name before marriage)	Family Name

Vargas-Gonzalez	Pedro	E.
Last Name	First Name	Middle Initial

Cruz	Refugio	("Cuca")	Gómez
Family Name	First Name	(Nickname)	Maiden Name

nickname = informal, friendly name (not official)

full, true, and correct name = whole name without abbreviations and nicknames

B Write T for true and F for false. Correct the false sentences.

1. __F__ Your first name is your ~~family~~ given name.

2. ___ Your last name is your given name.

3. ___ Some people have hyphenated first or last names.

4. ___ An initial is the last letter of a first or last name.

5. ___ Only a married woman has a maiden name.

6. ___ "Bob" and "Bill" are examples of common nicknames.

7. ___ Patty T. Gonzalez is an example of a full, true, and correct name.

 **Walk around the classroom. Use these patterns to ask your classmates questions. Write the answers on the lines.**

What's your	first middle last	given maiden family	name?	How do you spell it?

What's your	full name, middle initial,	please?	Do you have a nickname?

Is that your	first middle last	first or last maiden or last former or present	name?

1. NAME ____
        First   Middle   Last

2. NAME ____
        Last   First   Middle Initial

3. ____
   Given Name   Middle Initial   Maiden Name   Family Name

4. ________________________   ________________________
   Last Name   First Name   Initial   Maiden or Former Names

5. ________________________   ________________________
   Family Name   Given Name   Middle Name   Nickname, if any

6. ________________________   ________________________
   Full Name   Former Name, if any

7. ____
   Full, True, and Correct Name

D   **Introduce two students to the class. Tell about their names.**

EXAMPLE: This is Maria Elena Sanchez de Parra. Maria is her first name, and Elena is her middle name, but she uses them together. Sanchez is her father's last name and Parra is her husband's last name. Her nickname is Mari.

 **Addresses and Telephone Numbers**

ADDRESS   1414   22nd St.   #18
          number   street name   apartment

          San Diego   CA   92123
          city   state   zip code

TELEPHONE   (619)   555-3107
            area code   number

St. = Street   Rd. = Road   Ave. = Avenue   Apt. = Apartment   Dr. = Drive
Blvd. = Boulevard   Pl. = Place   No. = Number   # = Number

Official U.S. Post Office Abbreviations for States

CA = California   MA = Massachusetts   NY = New York
FL = Florida   MI = Michigan   PA = Pennsylvania

F **This is an information game. Follow the instructions exactly.**

1. Choose any square on the left (1-12). Print the first letter of your name in it. Put the other letters of your full name in the squares to the right of the first square. Leave an empty space between names.

2. Print the numbers and letters of your street address in other squares, from left to right.

3. In the same way, print the letters of your city and state in other squares.

4. In the same way, print the numbers of your zip code, area code, and telephone numbers in other squares.

Game 1

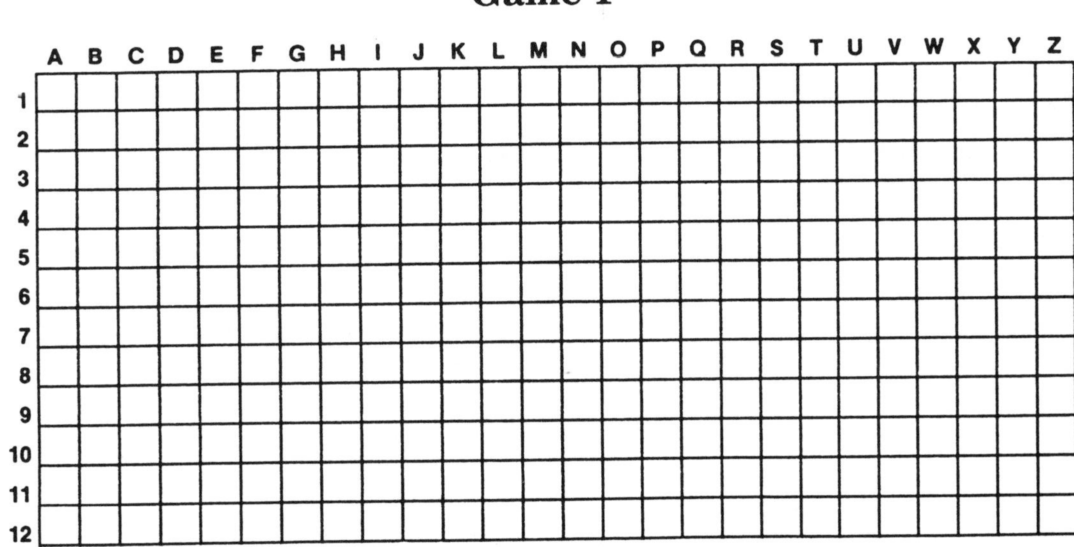

G **Now play the information game with a partner. Tell the location of the numbers and letters in your Game 1. Listen to the locations of your partner's numbers and letters and print them in Game 2.**

Game 2

H **On the lines, copy the information about your partner from Game 2.**

NAME ____

       Last   First   Middle   Maiden

ADDRESS____

       Number   Street Name   Apartment

City   State   Zip Code   Area Code   Telephone Number

I **Ask other classmates their names, addresses, and telephone numbers. Use this information to keep in touch.**

1. Name ___________________________   Telephone _________________

    Address ____

2. Name ___________________________   Telephone _________________

    Address ____

Module 1B: Biographic and Other Information

A Biographic Information

U.S. Department of Justice
Immigration and Naturalization Service

FORM G-325A
BIOGRAPHIC INFORMATION

OMB No. 1115-0066
Approval expires 4-30-85

(Family name)	(First name)	(Middle name)	MALE / ☑FEMALE	BIRTHDATE(Mo.-Day-Yr.)	NATIONALITY	FILE NUMBER
Farías	Eva	Maria	☑FEMALE	3-11-58	Colombian	A 92971062

ALL OTHER NAMES USED (Including names by previous marriages)
Eva Maria Uribe - Parra

CITY AND COUNTRY OF BIRTH
Bogotá, Colombia

SOCIAL SECURITY NO. (If any) 395-08-1041

	FAMILY NAME	FIRST NAME	DATE, CITY AND COUNTRY OF BIRTH(If known)	CITY AND COUNTRY OF RESIDENCE.
FATHER	Uribe	Manuel	2-7-34 Cali, Colombia	Bogotá, Colombia
MOTHER(Maiden name)	Parra	Stella	5-5-39 Lima, Peru	Bogotá, Colombia

HUSBAND(If none, so state) OR WIFE — FAMILY NAME (For wife, give maiden name)	FIRST NAME	BIRTHDATE	CITY & COUNTRY OF BIRTH	DATE OF MARRIAGE	PLACE OF MARRIAGE
Farías	Carlos	8-20-59	N.Y.C. USA	7-16-85	El Paso, TEXAS

FORMER HUSBANDS OR WIVES(If none, so state) FAMILY NAME (For wife, give maiden name)	FIRST NAME	BIRTHDATE	DATE & PLACE OF MARRIAGE	DATE AND PLACE OF TERMINATION OF MARRIAGE
None				

APPLICANT'S RESIDENCE LAST FIVE YEARS. LIST PRESENT ADDRESS FIRST.

STREET AND NUMBER	CITY	PROVINCE OR STATE	COUNTRY	FROM MONTH	FROM YEAR	TO MONTH	TO YEAR
8057 Hillcrest Dr.	Los Angeles	CA	U.S.A.	8	88	PRESENT TIME	
1109 52 nd St. # 212	El Paso	TX	U.S.A.	10	85	8	88
446 Rio Hondo Pl.	El Paso	TX	U.S.A.	2	83	10	85

APPLICANT'S LAST ADDRESS OUTSIDE THE UNITED STATES OF MORE THAN ONE YEAR

STREET AND NUMBER	CITY	PROVINCE OR STATE	COUNTRY	FROM MONTH	FROM YEAR	TO MONTH	TO YEAR
None							

APPLICANT'S EMPLOYMENT LAST FIVE YEARS. (IF NONE, SO STATE.) LIST PRESENT EMPLOYMENT FIRST

FULL NAME AND ADDRESS OF EMPLOYER	OCCUPATION (SPECIFY)	FROM MONTH	FROM YEAR	TO MONTH	TO YEAR
Green Onion Restaurant, 400 Cebolla Ave., Los Angeles, CA	Cook	10	88	PRESENT TIME	
The Tulip Cafe, 2066 Flower Blvd., EL PASO, TX	Waitress	5	84	5	85

Show below last occupation abroad if not shown above. (Include all information requested above.)

			FROM MONTH	FROM YEAR	TO MONTH	TO YEAR
La Luna record store Calle 42 #63 Bogota Colombia	Salesclerk	9	77	12	82

THIS FORM IS SUBMITTED IN CONNECTION WITH APPLICATION FOR:
☑ NATURALIZATION   ☐ STATUS AS PERMANENT RESIDENT
☐ OTHER (SPECIFY):

Are all copies legible? ☑ Yes

SIGNATURE OF APPLICANT   *Eva Maria Farias*   DATE 11-17-90

IF YOUR NATIVE ALPHABET IS IN OTHER THAN ROMAN LETTERS, WRITE YOUR NAME IN YOUR NATIVE ALPHABET IN THIS SPACE:

PENALTIES: SEVERE PENALTIES ARE PROVIDED BY LAW FOR KNOWINGLY AND WILLFULLY FALSIFYING OR CONCEALING A MATERIAL FACT.

APPLICANT: BE SURE TO PUT YOUR NAME AND ALIEN REGISTRATION NUMBER IN THE BOX OUTLINED BY HEAVY BORDER BELOW.

COMPLETE THIS BOX (Family name)	(Given name)	(Middle name)	(Alien registration number)
Farías	Eva	Maria	A- 92971062

B Answer the questions with information from the form in A.

1. What's the applicant's last name? ___FARIAS___

2. How old is she now? ____________ When is her birthday? ____________

3. What's her nationality? ____________

4. Where was she born? ____________

5. Does she have a social security number? ____________

6. Is she married? ____________ How long has she been married? ____________

7. Where did she get married? ____________ When? ____________

8. What's her husband's full name? ____________

9. What's his date of birth? ____________ Where was he born? ____________

10. Has her present marriage ended? ____________

11. Was she married before? ____________

12. What city and state does she live in now? ____________

13. When did she move there? ____________

14. What was her last address in El Paso, Texas? ____________

15. How long did she live in Texas? ____________

16. Has she lived outside the United States for more than one year in the last five years? ____________

17. How many jobs has she had in the United States? ____________

18. What is her present occupation? ____________

19. How long ago did she leave her last job? ____________

20. Where did she work as a waitress? ____________

21. How long was she a salesclerk? ____________

22. Is this application for status as a permanent resident? ____________

23. Is her native language in other than Roman letters? ____________

24. How long ago did she fill out the application? ____________

25. Is she a U.S. citizen now? ____________

C **To fill out the application form in D, you are going to interview a partner. What questions will you ask? Write them here.**

1. What's your last name?   Your first name?
   Do you have a middle name?
2. When were you born?

 **Work in pairs. Ask your partner your questions from C and other necessary questions. Use the information to fill out this form. (To get the real form, you can contact your local I.N.S. office.)**

U.S. Department of Justice
Immigration and Naturalization Service

FORM G-325A
BIOGRAPHIC INFORMATION

OMB No. 1115-0066
Approval expires 4-30-85

(Family name) (First name) (Middle name)	☐ MALE ☐ FEMALE	BIRTHDATE(Mo.-Day-Yr.)	NATIONALITY	FILE NUMBER A
ALL OTHER NAMES USED (Including names by previous marriages)		CITY AND COUNTRY OF BIRTH		SOCIAL SECURITY NO. (If any)

	FAMILY NAME	FIRST NAME	DATE, CITY AND COUNTRY OF BIRTH(If known)	CITY AND COUNTRY OF RESIDENCE.
FATHER				
MOTHER(Maiden name)				

HUSBAND(If none, so state) OR WIFE	FAMILY NAME (For wife, give maiden name)	FIRST NAME	BIRTHDATE	CITY & COUNTRY OF BIRTH	DATE OF MARRIAGE	PLACE OF MARRIAGE

FORMER HUSBANDS OR WIVES(if none, so state)

FAMILY NAME (For wife, give maiden name)	FIRST NAME	BIRTHDATE	DATE & PLACE OF MARRIAGE	DATE AND PLACE OF TERMINATION OF MARRIAGE

APPLICANT'S RESIDENCE LAST FIVE YEARS. LIST PRESENT ADDRESS FIRST.

STREET AND NUMBER	CITY	PROVINCE OR STATE	COUNTRY	FROM MONTH	YEAR	TO MONTH	YEAR
						PRESENT TIME	

APPLICANT'S LAST ADDRESS OUTSIDE THE UNITED STATES OF MORE THAN ONE YEAR

STREET AND NUMBER	CITY	PROVINCE OR STATE	COUNTRY	FROM MONTH	YEAR	TO MONTH	YEAR

APPLICANT'S EMPLOYMENT LAST FIVE YEARS. (IF NONE, SO STATE.) LIST PRESENT EMPLOYMENT FIRST

FULL NAME AND ADDRESS OF EMPLOYER	OCCUPATION(SPECIFY)	FROM MONTH	YEAR	TO MONTH	YEAR
				PRESENT TIME	

Show below last occupation abroad if not shown above. (Include all information requested above.)

THIS FORM IS SUBMITTED IN CONNECTION WITH APPLICATION FOR: ☐ NATURALIZATION ☐ STATUS AS PERMANENT RESIDENT ☐ OTHER (SPECIFY):	SIGNATURE OF APPLICANT	DATE

Are all copies legible? ☐ Yes	IF YOUR NATIVE ALPHABET IS IN OTHER THAN ROMAN LETTERS, WRITE YOUR NAME IN YOUR NATIVE ALPHABET IN THIS SPACE:

PENALTIES: SEVERE PENALTIES ARE PROVIDED BY LAW FOR KNOWINGLY AND WILLFULLY FALSIFYING OR CONCEALING A MATERIAL FACT.

APPLICANT: BE SURE TO PUT YOUR NAME AND ALIEN REGISTRATION NUMBER IN THE BOX OUTLINED BY HEAVY BORDER BELOW.

COMPLETE THIS BOX (Family name)	(Given name)	(Middle name)	(Alien registration number)

 **Use the information from the form in D to tell the class about your partner.**

EXAMPLES: My partner's name is Lin Chieh. She's over twenty-five years old. Her nationality is Chinese, but she was born in Japan.

Symbols and Holidays UNIT **2**

Module 2A: American Symbols

A The Flag of the United States

1. 
This is the British (English) flag. Before the American Revolution, it was the flag of the thirteen American colonies.

2. 
This was the "Great Union Flag." It was the flag of the American army during the Revolutionary War. The flag of England was in the corner. The red and white stripes were symbols for the thirteen American colonies.

3. 
Some people say that Betsy Ross made the first American flag. In the corner, there were thirteen white stars in a field of blue. The new flag also had seven red stripes and six white stripes.

4. 
During the War of 1812 the flag had fifteen stars and fifteen stripes for the fifteen states. After a battle Francis Scott Key wrote a song about the American flag. The "Star-Spangled Banner" became the national anthem of the United States.

5. 
The United States grew and admitted more states to the Union. Now the flag has thirteen stripes for the thirteen original colonies and fifty stars for the fifty states.

6. 
American citizens and immigrants sometimes recite the Pledge of Allegiance to the flag. The pledge is a promise of loyalty to the United States.

THE PLEDGE OF ALLEGIANCE

"I pledge allegiance to the Flag of the United States of America and to the Republic for which it stands, one Nation, under God, indivisible, with liberty and justice for all."

 Write T for true and F for False. Correct the false sentences.

1. __T__ Before the American Revolution, the British flag was the flag of the thirteen American colonies.
2. _____ The Great Union flag was the flag of England during the Revolutionary War.
3. _____ Some people say that Abraham Lincoln made the first American flag.
4. _____ The "Star-Spangled Banner" is a song about the Liberty Bell and the Statue of Liberty.
5. _____ The flag of the United States now has thirteen stars for the American colonies and fifty stripes for the fifty states.
6. _____ The Pledge of Allegiance is a promise of loyalty to the United States.

 Write the words from the box.

blue	stars	colonies	Revolution
white	stripes	Union	anthem

The British flag was the flag of the thirteen American (1) __colonies__ before the American (2) ______________ . During the Revolutionary War, the red and (3) ______________ stripes were symbols of these colonies on the Great (4) ______________ flag. The first American flag had thirteen (5) ______________ in a field of (6) ______________ . In the War of 1812, the flag had fifteen stars and (7) ______________ . Now the "Star-Spangled Banner" is the national (8) ______________ of the United States.

D Number the flags 1–5 in time order. Tell about each flag.

☐   ☐   ☐   ☐   ☐

E   More American Symbols

1. 
The delegates of the thirteen American colonies planned the Declaration of Independence, and Thomas Jefferson wrote it. The document declared the independence (separation) of the colonies from England.

2. 
Congress adopted the Declaration of Independence, and the delegates signed the document on July 4, 1776. The Liberty Bell in the State House in Philadelphia rang out on that day.

3. 
The French gave the Statue of Liberty to the United States as a symbol of friendship. Now it is a symbol of freedom for new immigrants to this country.

4. 
The American eagle is the official emblem (symbol) of the United States. It appears on the Presidential flag and on some coins.

5. 
The donkey and the elephant first appeared in political cartoons. They are symbols for the Democratic and Republican Parties.

6.
Uncle Sam has the initials U.S. He originally appeared in political cartoons and is an unofficial symbol of the U.S. government.

F   Match the sentence parts. Write the letters on the lines.

1. __C__ The Liberty Bell is the symbol of

2. _____ The Statue of Liberty is the symbol of

3. _____ The American eagle is the symbol of

4. _____ The donkey and the elephant are symbols of

5. _____ Uncle Sam is the symbol of

a. the United States on the Presidential flag and some coins.

b. the U.S. government.

c. the Declaration of Independence.

d. the two major political parties.

e. freedom for immigrants to the United States.

G   Write **T** for true and **F** for false. Correct the false sentences.

1. __F__   ~~George Washington~~ *Thomas Jefferson* wrote the Declaration of Independence.

2. _____   The document declared the separation and freedom of the thirteen colonies from England.

3. _____   The delegates of the thirteen original colonies signed the Declaration of Independence, and the Liberty Bell rang out in Philadelphia on July 4, 1776.

4. _____   The people of England gave the Statue of Liberty to the United States as a symbol of the President.

5. _____   The Democratic donkey is the official emblem of the United States.

6. _____   The donkey, the elephant, and Uncle Sam originally appeared in political cartoons.

H   With your class, learn and sing the "Star-Spangled Banner."

The Star-Spangled Banner

Module 2B: Thanksgiving and Independence Day

A Thanksgiving Day

1. 

The English Puritans were trying to "purify" the Church of England, but finally they formed their own church. They left England and went to Holland and then to America. They became "Pilgrims" because they were travelers in search of religious freedom.

2. 

In the fall of 1620 the Pilgrims crossed the Atlantic Ocean on their ship, the Mayflower. The trip was very difficult, and many people got sick. But while they were on the crowded ship, the Pilgrims agreed on a form of government for their new colony. This agreement, the Mayflower Compact, established the principles of voting and majority rule.

3. 

Finally on December 22 the travelers landed at Plymouth, Massachusetts. There was not enough food for the long, cold winter, and many settlers died. Then some friendly Indians, Samoset, Chief Massasoit, and Squanto, showed the Pilgrims how to hunt, fish, and plant corn, beans, and other foods. Because of their help, the Plymouth settlers had a good harvest the next fall.

4. 

Governor William Bradford declared some special days of thanksgiving. The Pilgrims and the Indians had a three-day feast of deer, wild turkey, and fish. There were also nuts, wild fruits, cranberries, corn, beans, pumpkins, and other foods. The first Thanksgiving celebration was a great success.

5. 

President Abraham Lincoln established Thanksgiving as an official national holiday. Now every year on the fourth Thursday of November American families and friends gather, have a feast, and give thanks. Some traditional Thanksgiving foods are turkey, dressing, sweet potatoes, cranberry sauce, and pumpkin pie.

 B Match the phrases. Write the letters on the lines.

1. __b__ the Pilgrims
2. ___ the Mayflower
3. ___ the Mayflower Compact
4. ___ Plymouth, Massachusetts
5. ___ Samoset, Squanto, and Massasoit
6. ___ William Bradford
7. ___ deer, wild turkey, corn, beans, pumpkins, and cranberries
8. ___ the fourth Thursday in November
9. ___ turkey, dressing, sweet potatoes, cranberry sauce, and pumpkin pie

a. some friendly Indians
b. the English Puritans
c. the governor of the Plymouth settlement
d. the ship of the Pilgrims
e. the official day of the national holiday of Thanksgiving
f. the settlement of the Pilgrims
g. the Pilgrims' agreement about government in their settlement
h. some foods at the first Thanksgiving feast
i. some traditional Thanksgiving foods today

C Write T for true and F for false. Correct the false sentences.

1. ___ The Puritans broke away from the Church of England and formed their own church.
2. ___ The Pilgrims were travelers in search of gold and adventure.
3. ___ The Pilgrims came to America in the seventeenth century.
4. ___ On the ship the Pilgrims established the government principle of separation of church and state.
5. ___ Their first winter in Plymouth, Massachusetts was very difficult.
6. ___ Then the settlers had a good harvest because some friendly Indians taught them about the land.
7. ___ Governor William Bradford declared a special day to celebrate the independence of their colony from England.
8. ___ Now Thanksgiving is an official national feast day for families and friends.

D   Independence Day

During the Revolutionary War some of the American settlers wanted to declare the independence of the colonies from British rule. At that time the Second Continental Congress was acting as the central government of the thirteen colonies. The Congress asked Thomas Jefferson to write the Declaration of Independence.

This historic document contains several important principles of American government. It says that "all men are created equal," all people have the right to "life, liberty, and the pursuit of happiness," and government can exist only with "the consent of the governed."

Congress adopted the Declaration of Independence, and the delegates of the thirteen colonies, now new states, signed the document on July 4, 1776. The Liberty Bell in the State House of Philadelphia rang out that day.

Now Americans celebrate the Fourth of July as the birthday of the United States. Independence Day is an official national holiday. People have picnics, and there are often parades, speeches, and fireworks. American flags are everywhere.

E   Write the words from the box.

principles of government	the Declaration of Independence
thirteen new states	the Revolutionary War
British rule	the Liberty Bell
picnics, parades, speeches, and fireworks	Independence Day

During (1) **the Revolutionary War** some colonists wanted to declare the independence of the colonies from (2) _______________________. The Congress asked Thomas Jefferson to write (3) _______________________. This document contains several important (4) _______________________ _______________________. Delegates of the (5) _______________________ signed the document on July 4, 1776, and (6) _______________________ rang out. Now the Fourth of July is American (7) _______________________. Americans celebrate with (8) _______________________ _______________________.

Answer these questions about the two American holidays.

Thanksgiving

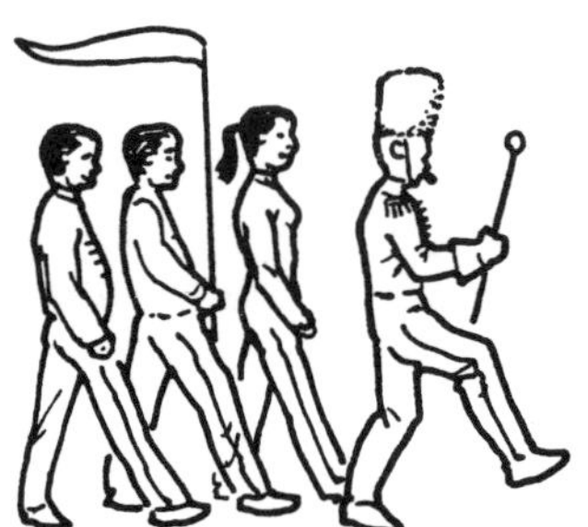

Independence Day

	Thanksgiving	Independence Day
1. When did the holiday begin?	*in the fall of 1621*	
2. What group(s) of people began the holiday?		
3. What did these people do?		
4. What is the meaning of the holiday?		
5. When do Americans celebrate this holiday now?		
6. What do people do to celebrate this holiday?		

Module 2C: More National Holidays

A Legal Holidays in the United States

Holiday	Date of Celebration	Calendar Date	Purpose
New Year's Day	January 1	January 1	the celebration of the calendar new year
Martin Luther King, Jr. Day	the third Monday in January	January 15	the remembrance of the civil rights leader's birthday
Presidents Day	the third Monday in February	February 12 (Lincoln) February 22 (Washington)	a birthday celebration for two famous Presidents (See Module 3A.)
Memorial Day	the last Monday in May	May 30	the remembrance of past wars and a day to visit military and family graves
Independence Day	July 4	July 4	the birthday of the United States (See Module 2B.)
Labor Day	the first Monday in September	the first Monday in September	a celebration of the industrial spirit and the dignity of work
Columbus Day	the second Monday in October	October 12	the remembrance of Christopher Columbus and his spirit of achievement
Veterans Day	November 11	November 11	the honoring of Americans who fought in wars and a a promise to work for peace
Thanksgiving Day	the fourth Thursday in November	the fourth Thursday in November	a day to gather friends, feast, and give thanks (See Module 2B.)
Christmas Day	December 25	December 25	the celebration of the birth of Jesus Christ

B Make sentences about the information in A. You can use these sentence patterns.

1. The calendar date of _______________ is _______________, but Americans really celebrate
         (holiday)   (date)
   it on _______________.
      (date)
2. The purpose of the holiday is _______________.

 C Martin Luther King, Jr. Day

1.

Dr. Martin Luther King, Jr. was born on January 15, 1929. He became a Baptist minister. In 1956, because blacks had to sit in the back of buses, he led a 381-day boycott of (refusal to use) the bus system in Montgomery, Alabama. He was the leader of many protests in the 1950s and 60s. The police often arrested King's followers or used dogs and fire hoses to oppose them. On August 28, 1963, King joined 200,000 black and white protesters called Freedom Marchers at the Lincoln Memorial in Washington, D.C. to support new laws for civil rights. There, his "I have a dream..." speech moved the nation.

2.

Martin Luther King, Jr. used only peaceful methods to fight against unjust laws because he opposed violence. He said that it was important to change laws but even more important to change minds and hearts. He helped blacks win their legal rights and made progress in the cause of integration (the mixing of the races) in schools, churches, and public places. King won the Nobel Peace Prize in 1964. But on April 4, 1968, he was assassinated in Memphis, Tennessee. Now on Martin Luther King, Jr. Day Americans remember a great man and promise to work hard for civil rights.

D Write T for true and F for false. Correct the false sentences.

1. ___ Martin Luther King, Jr. was a leader in the struggle for civil rights and equality for black people.

2. ___ In 1956 he led a famous boycott of the school system because blacks couldn't become teachers.

3. ___ The police always supported the marches of his followers because King opposed violence.

4. ___ There was a famous march for freedom and civil rights in Washington, D.C. in 1963.

5. ___ King did not believe in integration because he wanted the separation of the races.

6. ___ He won the Nobel Peace Prize in 1964 but was assassinated in 1968.

E **Work in groups of four. Each of you studies the information about a different one of these four holidays. In turn, summarize your information in your own words for the group.**

1. 

Memorial Day, first called Decoration Day, began after the Civil War to honor the war dead of both the North and the South. Today, patriotic Americans remember the dead soldiers of all American wars, as well as their own family members who died. People decorate graves with flags and flowers. They watch military parades. Some watch the Indianapolis 500, one of America's greatest auto races.

2. 

Labor Day celebrates the industrial spirit of the United States. It was the idea of Labor leader Peter S. McGuire over one hundred years ago. Today, Labor Day represents the idea that the success of the individual and the nation comes from hard work. The holiday marks the end of summer and the beginning of the school year. Families and friends enjoy the three-day weekend with trips, sports, or relaxation.

3. 

Columbus Day honors the achievement of an Italian explorer, Christopher Columbus. Columbus knew the world was round, and he wanted to sail to the other side. Finally, King Ferdinand and Queen Isabella of Spain agreed to support him. On October 12, 1492, this European sailor discovered a new world. Today, patriotic citizens remember Columbus, and school children learn that education and hard work are important for progress.

4. 

Veterans Day, once called Armistice Day, began after World War I. At 11:00 a.m. on November 11, 1919, Americans stopped for two minutes of silence to honor the courage of those who died in that war. Today on this day of remembrance, citizens honor veterans (former soldiers) still living, as well as the dead of all American wars. Patriotic Americans watch memorial parades and attend quiet ceremonies.

 **Which holiday is each sentence about? Write M for Memorial Day, L for Labor Day, C for Columbus Day, and V for Veterans Day. Sentence 9 has two answers.**

1. __C__   On this day in 1492, an explorer from Italy, with the support of the King and Queen of Spain, discovered a new world.

2. ___   This holiday was first called Armistice Day.

3. ___   This holiday was first called Decoration Day.

4. ___   It began after the Civil War in remembrance of the dead on both sides.

5. ___   This holiday is in honor of the industrial spirit of the U.S. because it represents the idea that all work has dignity.

6. ___   It began on November 11, 1919, in remembrance of the dead soldiers of World War I.

7. ___   A labor leader had the idea for this celebration over 100 years ago.

8. ___   On this patriotic holiday, school children learn the importance of education and hard work for progress.

9. ___ ___   Today on this day of remembrance, Americans honor veterans and the dead of past wars with parades and ceremonies.

10. ___   Today, people decorate graves, watch military parades, and may see the Indianapolis 500 on this holiday.

11. ___   It is the last three-day weekend of summer, before school begins, and people use it to relax.

12. ___   This holiday is in honor of the achievement of a European explorer.

 **Is there a holiday to honor a famous person in your native culture? In small groups, tell about it. Answer these questions:**

1. What is the history of the holiday? Why and when did it begin?

2. What is the meaning of the holiday?

3. Who celebrates the holiday?

3. Where, when, and how do they usually celebrate it?

What similarities did you find in two or more holidays of different cultures? Tell the class.

H **Repeat Exercise G, but this time talk about a patriotic holiday.**

Americans

Module 3A: Famous Presidents

A **Work in groups of four. Each of you studies the information about a different one of the four presidents. In turn, summarize your information in your own words for the group.**

1.

Before the United States won independence from British rule, George Washington was a farmer in the colony of Virginia. He served as a military leader in the Revolutionary War. The colonists trusted him because he did not want power for himself. He wanted all the states and the people to work together as one. He wanted the government to serve the people well.

Washington said that power should belong to institutions, not to men. He also said that people could understand the U.S. Constitution in many ways, not just one. He did not think that the United States should have strong ties with other countries.

George Washington was the first President of the United States from 1789 to 1796. He is often called "the Father of Our Country."

2.

Thomas Jefferson could do many things. As a young man, he was a farmer and a lawyer in Virginia. He was also a scientist, an inventor, a philosopher, and an architect. He designed his own home, called Montecello. He could communicate in French, Italian, Spanish, Latin, and Greek.

Many of Jefferson's ideas became basic principles of the government of the United States. For example, he believed that "all men are created equal" (are born the same and should receive the same treatment under the law). He also said that power must come from "the consent of the governed" (the voters, not the leaders). He wanted free elections, a free press, and free speech.

Thomas Jefferson held many important government jobs. He was Ambassador to France, Secretary of State (under George Washington), Vice President (under John Adams), and the third President of the United States, from 1801 to 1809. As President, Jefferson bought the huge Louisiana Territory for the United States from France.

3.

Abraham Lincoln grew up in Kentucky in a log cabin. He couldn't go to school, so he taught himself. He became a lawyer. Friends called him "Honest Abe." As a delegate from Illinois, he served in Congress from 1847 to 1849. Lincoln was against slavery and gave some famous speeches about his ideas when he was running for the Senate.

In 1861 Abraham Lincoln became the sixteenth President of the United States. He wanted the states of the Union to work together as one country, but he had to lead the North against the South in the Civil War. Some people thought that Lincoln was too strong as President because he used power that the Constitution did not give him.

President Lincoln freed the slaves with the Emancipation Proclamation. He had a plan to bring the South back into the Union after the Civil War, but he couldn't carry out the plan because he was assassinated. In 1865 an actor named John Wilkes Booth shot Abraham Lincoln.

4.

John F. Kennedy was President for only three years, from 1961 to 1963, but his personality and ideas changed America. He was both the first Roman Catholic and the youngest President in the history of the country. He set clear goals for America. For example, he promised that the United States would land a man on the moon before 1970.

Kennedy supported the ideas of Martin Luther King, Jr. and fought for civil rights, fair housing, and programs to stop poverty. He asked Congress for more money for education and medical care for elderly people.

Kennedy was against Communism. For example, when the Soviet Union put missiles in Cuba, he sent U.S. ships to surround the island. But he believed that the best way to fight Communism was not by sending armies but by attacking poverty and injustice. He organized the Alliance for Progress to help the countries of Latin America. He started the Peace Corps and sent Americans to over sixty countries in Africa, Asia, and South America. These young volunteers worked and lived with the people, built schools, and taught farmers more modern methods.

Kennedy was a man for the future. He worked to stop the testing of nuclear weapons. But on November 22, 1963, he was assassinated.

B Which President is each sentence about? Write the first initial of his last name on the line.

W = Washington   J = Jefferson   L = Lincoln   K = Kennedy

1. __J__ This farmer and lawyer from Virginia was also a scientist, an inventor, a philosopher, and an architect, and he knew many languages.

2. ___ The colonists trusted this farmer from the colony of Virginia because he did not want power for himself.

3. ___ This young Roman Catholic was President for only three years because he was assassinated in 1963.

4. ___ He served as a military leader in the fight of the colonists for independence from British rule.

5. ___ This honest man taught himself and became a lawyer and a Congressman from Illinois.

6. ___ He was against slavery but wanted the states of the North and South to work together as a nation.

7. ___ Many of his ideas (for example, about equality, "the consent of the governed," free press, and free speech) are basic principles of the government of the United States.

8. ___ He was an Ambassador, Secretary of State, and Vice President before he became the third President of the United States.

9. ___ He was a man for the future, and one of his goals was to land a man on the moon before 1970.

10. ___ As the sixteenth President, he used power that was not given by the Constitution when he led the northern states in the Civil War.

11. ___ He did not think the United States should have strong ties to other nations.

12. ___ He bought the Louisiana Territory for the United States from France.

13. ___ He is often called "the Father of Our Country."

14. ___ His Emancipation Proclamation freed the slaves, but he was assassinated before he bring the South back into the Union.

15. ___ He supported civil rights, fair housing, and programs to stop poverty, and he wanted more money for education and medical care for elderly people.

16. ___ He tried to stop Communism with the Alliance for Progress and the Peace Corps and was against nuclear weapons.

C   Which of the four Presidents said or wrote these famous quotes? Write their names on the lines. (The information in A will help you.)

George Washington   Thomas Jefferson   Abraham Lincoln   John F. Kennedy

1. _John F. Kennedy_ : "And so, my fellow Americans, ask not what your country can do for you: Ask what you can do for your country. My fellow citizens of the world: Ask not what America will do for you, but what together we can do for the freedom of man."

2. _______________ : "We hold these truths to be self evident, that all men are created equal, that they are endowed by their Creator with certain unalienable rights, that among these are life, liberty, and the pursuit of happiness."

3. _______________ : "It is our true policy to steer clear of permanent alliances, with any portion of the foreign world."

4. _______________ : "A house divided against itself cannot stand. I believe that this government cannot endure permanently half slave and half free."

D   In small groups, discuss the meanings of the quotes in C. On the lines, write the ideas in simpler language.

1. _Americans should work for America. Everyone should work for freedom._

2. ____

3. ____

4. ____

E   In books, find other famous quotes by Presidents of the United States. Write them on the chalkboard and discuss their meanings as a class.

 **Module 3B:** The History of Immigration

A Work in pairs. Look only at this page. Tell your partner these facts about immigration history in order.

1. There were about twenty-five million "native Americans" (Indians) living in North and South America.

2. The English were the largest immigrant group to settle in North America. They were farmers, fishermen, and traders.

3. By the time of the American Revolution, there were also many immigrants from Scotland, Ireland, France, Holland, Germany, Sweden, and Poland. Most of these settlers were Protestants.

4. The Spanish settled mainly in the Southwest, especially California. They were managers, priests, and soldiers.

5. American slave traders captured black Africans and forced them to work on plantations in the United States.

B Now listen to your partner and number these facts 6–10 in correct time order.

___ After the Gold Rush in California, 100,000 poor Chinese came to work in mining camps and on the railroad.

___ The U.S. government abolished quotas for immigration from non-European nations. Today, most immigrants are from Asian and Latin American countries.

6 During the Industrial Revolution, about 3.5 million Irish Catholics left poverty and discrimination to work in America. They were coal miners and railroad and canal builders. At the same time, many Germans became farmers, laborers, and businessmen in the United States.

___ During the "Great Migration," twenty-five million Europeans of almost every nationality immigrated to America. They included Russian and Polish Jews, Slavic people from Eastern Europe, Italians, Greeks, Armenians, and Syrians. Canadians, Mexicans, and Central Americans came, too.

___ The United States welcomed thousands of refugees after the end of World War II.

 **Work in pairs. Look only at this page. Your partner will tell you some important facts about immigration history. Number them 1-5 in correct time order.**

___ American slave traders captured black Africans and forced them to work on plantations in the United States.

___ By the time of the American Revolution, there were also many immigrants from Scotland, Ireland, France, Holland, Germany, Sweden, and Poland. Most of these settlers were Protestants.

___ The English were the largest immigrant group to settle in North America. They were farmers, fishermen, and traders.

___ The Spanish settled mainly in the Southwest, especially California. They were managers, priests, and soldiers.

<u>1</u> There were about twenty-five million "native Americans" (Indians) living in North and South America.

B **Now tell your partner these facts about immigration history in order.**

6. During the Industrial Revolution, about 3.5 million Irish Catholics left poverty and discrimination to work in America. They were coal miners and railroad and canal builders. At the same time, many Germans became farmers, laborers, and businessmen in the United States.

7. After the Gold Rush in California, 100,000 poor Chinese came to work in mining camps and on the railroad.

8. During the "Great Migration," twenty-five million Europeans of almost every nationality immigrated to America. They included Russian and Polish Jews, Slavic people from Eastern Europe, Italians, Greeks, Armenians, and Syrians. Canadians, Mexicans, and Central Americans came, too.

9. The United States welcomed thousands of refugees after the end of World War II.

10. The U.S. government abolished quotas for immigration from non-European nations. Today, most immigrants are from Asian and Latin American countries.

1820 to 1880 | 1850 to 1870 | 1880 to 1930 | 1940's 1950's | 1960's 1970's

C Tell some important facts about immigration history. You can use these pictures for ideas.

D Changes in Immigration

The history of the United States is the history of immigration. Before 1880, the United States welcomed immigrants from all countries. Because Americans were moving west, factories in the East needed new workers. Most of these immigrants came from northern and western Europe, so they looked like born Americans, and their cultures were similar. The talents, spirit, and hard work of millions of immigrants built American farms, industry, and cities.

But then Americans began to worry about the influence and power of large groups of immigrants from cultures very different from their own. In the next century, the U.S. government passed many immigration acts. Before World War II, these laws limited immigration, especially from non-European nations. But after the war, new acts made it easier for refugees and immigrants to come to the United States.

E Write **T** for true or **F** for false. Correct the false sentences.

1. ___   The United States passed many laws to limit immigration before 1880.

2. ___   Many European immigrants came to work in the factories in the East.

3. ___   America needed the talents, spirit, and hard work of immigrants to grow.

4. ___   Born Americans probably accept immigrants from similar cultures more easily than immigrants from very different ones.

5. ___   America welcomed immigration before World War II, but after the war, new laws made it harder for refugees to come to the United States.

F   Immigration Law

YEAR	THE ACT OR LAW	THE EFFECT OF THE LAW
1882	The Chinese Exclusion Act	prohibited the Chinese from entering the country.
1907	T. Roosevelt's "Gentlemen's Agreement"	stopped Japanese laborers from coming to the United States.
1917	The Literacy Test Act	kept out illiterate immigrants (people unable to read or write in any language).
1924	An immigration act	set up a quota system (yearly limits on the numbers of immigrants from each country). The law allowed higher quotas for some nations than for others.
	The National Origins Act	excluded all Japanese, Chinese, and other Asians from the United States.
1948	The Displaced Persons Act	allowed 500,000 war victims to immigrate to the United States.
	The Fulbright Act	brought in scholars from around the world. Many of them stayed in this country.
1952	The McCarran-Walter Act	opened the United States to Asian immigration. But the quota system still discriminated against non-Europeans.
1953	The Refugee Relief Act	admitted over 200,000 refugees outside the quota system.
1965	An immigration act	set area quotas instead of national ones: 120,000 immigrants per year from the Western hemisphere (Canada and Central and South America) and 170,000 per year from the rest of the world.
1986	The Immigration Reform Control Act	gave amnesty to many illegal aliens and and allowed them to legalize their status. The law puts penalties on employers that hire employees without work authorization.

G   Make sentences about the information in F. You can use this sentence pattern.

EXAMPLE: In 1882, the Chinese Exclusion Act prohibited the Chinese from entering the country.

In ________, ____.
  (year)   (the act or law)

Module 3C: Historical Figures

A In groups or as a class, answer these questions about each picture: (1) Why do you think this person was famous? (2) What do you think this person did?

a 

John James Audubon
(1785-1851)

b 

Susan B. Anthony
(1820-1906)

c 

Clara Barton
(1821 - 1912)

d 

Cesar Chavez
(1927 -)

e 

Samuel Clemens
(1835 - 1910)

f 

Thomas A. Edison
(1847 - 1937)

g 

Duke Ellington
(1899 - 1974)

h 

Henry Ford
(1863 - 1947)

i 

Benjamin Franklin
(1706 - 1790)

j 

Hideyo Noguchi
(1876 - 1928)

k 

Eleanor Roosevelt
(1884 - 1962)

l 

Lawrence Welk
(1903 -)

 In correct time order, make sentences about the twelve people on the previous page with this pattern.

EXAMPLE: Benjamin Franklin lived from 1706 to 1790.

_________________________________ lived from __________ to ___________.
(name)   (year)   (year)

 Which person is each paragraph about? On the lines, write the letters of the pictures a–l from the previous page. You can check your answers on the next page.

1. __*i*__ This Founding Father of the United States was an example of "an ideal American." He left school at age ten but wrote, printed, and published books and newspapers. He studied science and invented useful things such as bifocal glasses, a stove, and the lightning rod. For the colonies, he printed money and served as Deputy Postmaster General. He helped write the Declaration of Independence and the U.S. Constitution. He often served as a diplomat to other nations.

2. ____ This immigrant loved nature. He painted pictures of all the known species (kinds) of North American birds. Today, a society named after him studies birds and works for their protection.

3. ____ This women's rights leader led the fight for women's suffrage (the right to vote). She also campaigned for prohibition (against the use of alcohol). She was against slavery before the Civil War and worked for Black rights after the war. The government arrested, tried, and convicted her because she tried to vote illegally.

4. ____ This "angel of the battlefield" helped wounded soldiers in wars in America and Europe. She began the American Red Cross. She got the United States to sign an international agreement about the treatment of the sick, wounded, and dead in battle and prisoners of war. Under her leadership, the Red Cross began to give aid to the victims of natural disasters, such as floods.

5. ____ This writer used the name Mark Twain. He learned to write through his work, travels, and reading. He used the language of ordinary people to write stories such as *Tom Sawyer* and *Huckleberry Finn*. He was also a newspaperman and spoke on many subjects, including the responsibility of the white man. He did not believe that whites should try to have power over other peoples.

6. ___ This inventor started work at age twelve. As a young man, he created and manufactured useful machines for stock brokers and telegraph services. After 1876, his research led to many useful inventions, such as the light bulb, movie projector, and phonograph.

7. ___ This businessman changed factory production in America with assembly-line methods to lower costs. He worked for the Edison Company in Detroit until 1899 and then began manufacturing automobiles. His earliest cars were the Model T and the Model A. In 1932, his company began to sell cars with eight-cylinder engines. For many years, he refused to allow unions in his factories, but he signed his first contract with the United Auto Workers (UAW) in 1941.

8. ___ This Japanese immigrant studied bacteria and snake venom (poison) in the laboratory. His work of twenty-five years at the Rockefeller Institute for Medical Research in New York led to discoveries about polio and other diseases and a vaccine for yellow fever. But when he was doing research in Africa, he got yellow fever and died of it.

9. ___ This wife of a famous President used her position to help humanity. She supported young people's organizations, child welfare, the improvement of housing, and equal rights for everyone. After her husband's death, she became a delegate to the United Nations. She was chairperson of the U.N. Commission on Human Rights and helped write the Universal Declaration of Human Rights.

10. ___ This creator of big band jazz wrote music, played piano, and led large orchestras. His music combined special sounds with the talents of great musicians. Besides big band music, he wrote for opera, ballets, Broadway shows, and films.

11. ___ This son of German immigrants learned English only after he left the farm at age twenty-one. He became a famous American T.V. host and big band leader. To his co-workers, he represents family-like co-operation, hard work, honesty, and healthy living. Today, he continues to encourage children to work hard to develop their talents and increase their chances for success.

12. ___ This union organizer began and continues to lead the United Farm Workers of America (UFW). In the 1960s, he led successful battles to help grape and lettuce pickers. Growers tried to stop him in the 1970s with their support of another union, the Teamsters, but the UFW won the right to organize and represent all field workers. In 1988 he led a fast (refusal to eat) and a grape boycott (refusal to buy) to call attention to the harmful effects of pesticides (insect poisons) on workers.

Answers to Exercise C: 1. i 2. a 3. b 4. c 5. e 6. f 7. h 8. j 9. k 10. g 11. l 12. d

D **Who are these facts about? On each line, write the name of one of the people from page 29.**

1. ___Henry Ford___ was an automobile manufacturer and the first to sell cars with eight-cylinder engines.

2. _______________ wrote newspaper stories and spoke on issues such as the responsibility of the white man toward other peoples. He was the author of Tom Sawyer, Huckleberry Finn, and other famous stories.

3. _______________ was the wife of a President. She worked for many causes. As a U.N. delegate, she was a leader in the fight for human rights.

4. _______________ led the battle for women's rights, especially the right to vote. She fought against slavery and for Black rights. She was for prohibition.

5. _______________ made discoveries about polio and other diseases. His work led to a vaccine for yellow fever.

6. _______________ was a Founding Father of the United States. He wrote, published, created useful inventions, worked on the Declaration of Independence and the U.S. Constitution, and was a diplomat to other countries.

7. _______________ loved nature and painted pictures of birds. A society named after him works to protect birds.

8. _______________ is a T.V. host and band leader. He continues to represent American values such as cooperation, hard work, honesty, and healthy living.

9. _______________ wrote jazz and music for opera, ballets, shows, and films. He was the creator of big band jazz.

10. _______________ started the American Red Cross. She worked to help the victims of wars and natural disasters.

11. _______________ created machines for stock brokers and telegraph services, the light bulb, the movie projector, the phonograph, and other useful inventions.

12. _______________ led the protests of field workers against grape and lettuce growers and began the United Farm Workers of America. He and his union continue to organize boycotts and protest the use of pesticides.

 **Turn back to page 29. In groups, tell one fact about each of the famous people in the pictures.**

 **Do you know facts about other famous American historical figures? Tell the class.**

Module 3D: Some Immigration Stories

A **Work in groups of four. Each of you studies a different one of these immigration stories. In turn, tell "your story" to the group.**

1.

Catherine Galligher is my name. I am Irish-born and a Catholic. In my native country, the Protestant English kept my brothers and me from getting the good-paying jobs in the city. Then the potato crop failed in all of Ireland. In 1849, I paid $25 to travel by ship to the United States. America was good to me. I worked as a maid in the house of a wealthy Boston family for twenty years. I also married an Irishman. He first laid tracks for the railroad and later became a union leader in Boston.

But life in the New World wasn't perfect. Many people discriminated against the Irish. For example, signs on stores and businesses said "No Irish need apply." In 1849, the secret "Know-Nothing Party" started to work against immigrant groups, especially Catholics. After 1887, the American Protective Association opposed us in the same way. But we Irish kept trying to succeed. We are proud of our great railroad and canal builders, as well as our writers and politicians.

2.

Although my family wanted to leave China for a long time, they couldn't enter the United States because of laws against Asian immigration. The Chinese Exclusion Act of 1882 kept the Chinese out of the country until World War II. In 1924, the National Origins Act excluded all Asians. I guess some Americans were worried about the influence and power of people from other countries. They didn't want foreigners to take their jobs or use public services, so the government limited the number of immigrants.

Anyway, in 1952, the McCarran-Walter Act allowed Asians to immigrate to the United States. I came here the next year. My name at birth was Ling Chiao, but I changed it to Charlie Ling because few Americans can pronounce my real name. Now I work as a shipping agent in San Pedro, California. The Immigration Act of 1965 abolished quotas for immigration from Asian nations, so now it will be easier for some of my relatives to come to America.

3.

My name is Yacob Wolf. I was born in Russia before it became the Soviet Union. In my native country, violent mobs of Russians burnt down my father's butcher shop and the community synagogue (place of worship). There is a long tradition of learning in my family, so my sisters and I were hoping to attend a university in Moscow and become writers and doctors. But Russian universities refused to admit us, so my whole family immigrated to the United States in 1910.

At first my father worked in a butcher shop in Chicago, Illinois. He bought his own store a few years later, and it soon became a small market. My mother opened a school for young girls. But not everything was perfect in our new country. My sister Elena couldn't enter Harvard University, even though her grades were perfect in high school, because no Jewish students were allowed. Happily, some excellent universities and colleges changed their policies in later years. Today both my sisters teach science, and I own a small publishing company in New York.

4.

I am Juan Rivera. My grandparents, Jose and Maria Sanchez, came to California from Oaxaca, Mexico, in 1920. For forty years, they picked vegetables and fruits from the fields and orchards of California. They were very poor, but they raised eleven children. The children helped their parents on the farms, so they couldn't go to school. But my mother, Rosa Sanchez, learned to read and finished high school at night. Later she finished college and learned the skills to be an accountant.

My mother married my father, Armando Rivera, in 1945. He is a lawyer. I'm glad my grandparents immigrated to the United States because everyone in my family used the opportunities here to give their children better lives. I am a flight engineer with the U.S. Space Program. I am thankful for my fine education and proud to be a third-generation Mexican-American.

Some of my cousins came to this country illegally in the 1970s, but the Immigration Reform and Control Act of 1986 allowed them to apply for legal status. Now they are temporary residents of the United States. They are studying English and American history and government so they can become permanent residents and later U.S. citizens. They are happy and thankful for the opportunity to improve their lives.

B **Write T for true and F for false. (You can look back at the stories on the previous two pages for facts about immigration.) Correct the false sentences.**

1. ___ Catherine Galligher is a typical Russian Jewish name.

2. ___ In Ireland in the 1800s, the Protestants often discriminated against the Catholics.

3. ___ Many Irish came to the United States in the 1840s because the clothing industry failed.

4. ___ European immigrants in the 1800s paid thousands of dollars to travel to the New World by plane.

5. ___ Many Irishmen build railroads or canals or became writers or politicians.

6. ___ There was no discrimination against the Irish in the United States because they are white and Catholic.

7. ___ The secret "Know-Nothing Party" and the American Protective Association worked to increase immigration from European countries.

8. ___ Americans don't worry about influence, power, or jobs, so there have never been any laws against Asian immigrants.

9. ___ The Chinese Exclusion Act of 1882 and the National Origins Act of 1924 limited immigration to the United States.

10. ___ Some immigrants change their real names when they come to America.

11. ___ In 1965 an immigration law abolished quotas (limits on numbers of immigrants from certain countries).

12. ___ In the early 1900s, there was discrimination and violence against Jewish people in Russia.

13. ___ Famous American universities, such as Harvard, have refused to admit some groups of people.

14. ___ Many Mexican workers have picked vegetables and fruit in the fields and orchards of California.

15. ___ America is a land of educational opportunity.

16. ___ Many people who entered the United States illegally have become legal residents and may become citizens.

 **To begin to tell your own "immigration story" or the story of a friend or relative, write the answers to these questions.**

EXAMPLE: Before I came to the United States, there was a revolution in my country. I was teaching at a high school when the new government came into power. The military leaders didn't like my political ideas, so I lost my job.

1. What was happening in your (his, her) native country before you (he, she) came to the United States?

2. What were you (he, she) doing at that time?

3. When and how did you (he, she) come to the United States?

4. Why did you (he, she) immigrate to the United States?

5. What happened to you (him, her) or what did you (he, she) do when you first got here?

6. How has your (his, her) life changed since your arrival in this country?

7. How do you think your (his, her) life here will change in the future?

D **In pairs, tell your own immigration story or the story of your friend or relative from C. Your partner will ask you questions. Make sure your partner understands your story. Then listen to his or her story and make sure you understand.**

E **With your partner, form a group of four with another pair of students. Tell your partner's immigration story to the group. Your partner will help you tell it correctly.**

Geography

Module 4A: The Geography of the United States

A The Geography of the United States

The United States is the fourth largest country in the world in land area. Forty-eight of the fifty states are in the middle of the North American continent between the Atlantic Ocean on the east and the Pacific Ocean on the west. It is about 3000 miles (4800 kilometers) from the east coast to the west coast and about 1500 miles (2400 kilometers) from the Canadian border on the north to the Mexican border on the south. The island state of Hawaii is in the Pacific Ocean, and the state of Alaska is northwest of Canada.

The map on the next page shows the geography of the United States. The two main mountain ranges run north and south—the Appalachian Mountains in the eastern part of the United States and the Rocky Mountains in the west. Between them are the Great Plains. There is another mountain chain west of the Rockies—the Sierra Nevada and the Cascade range.

The longest river in the United States is the Mississippi. The Missouri and Ohio Rivers flow into the Mississippi, and the Mississippi flows south into the Gulf of Mexico. The major rivers in the western part of the United States are the Colorado and the Rio Grande. The highest mountains of the Rockies form the Continental Divide. Rivers to the east of the divide flow east, and rivers to the west of it flow into the Pacific Ocean.

The Great Lakes on the northern border of the country are Lake Superior, Lake Michigan, Lake Huron, Lake Erie, and Lake Ontario. The Great Salt Lake is in a desert area in the western part of the United States. The Mojave, the Gila, and the Painted Deserts are in the southwestern part of the country.

B Write O for oceans, M for mountains, R for rivers, L for lakes, and D for deserts.

1. __M__ the Appalachians	8. ___ the Ohio
2. ___ the Atlantic	9. ___ the Pacific
3. ___ the Sierra Nevada	10. ___ the Rockies
4. ___ Superior	11. ___ the Cascade Range
5. ___ the Mojave and the Gila	12. ___ the Missouri
6. ___ Michigan and Huron	13. ___ the Mississippi
7. ___ the Colorado	14. ___ Erie and Ontario

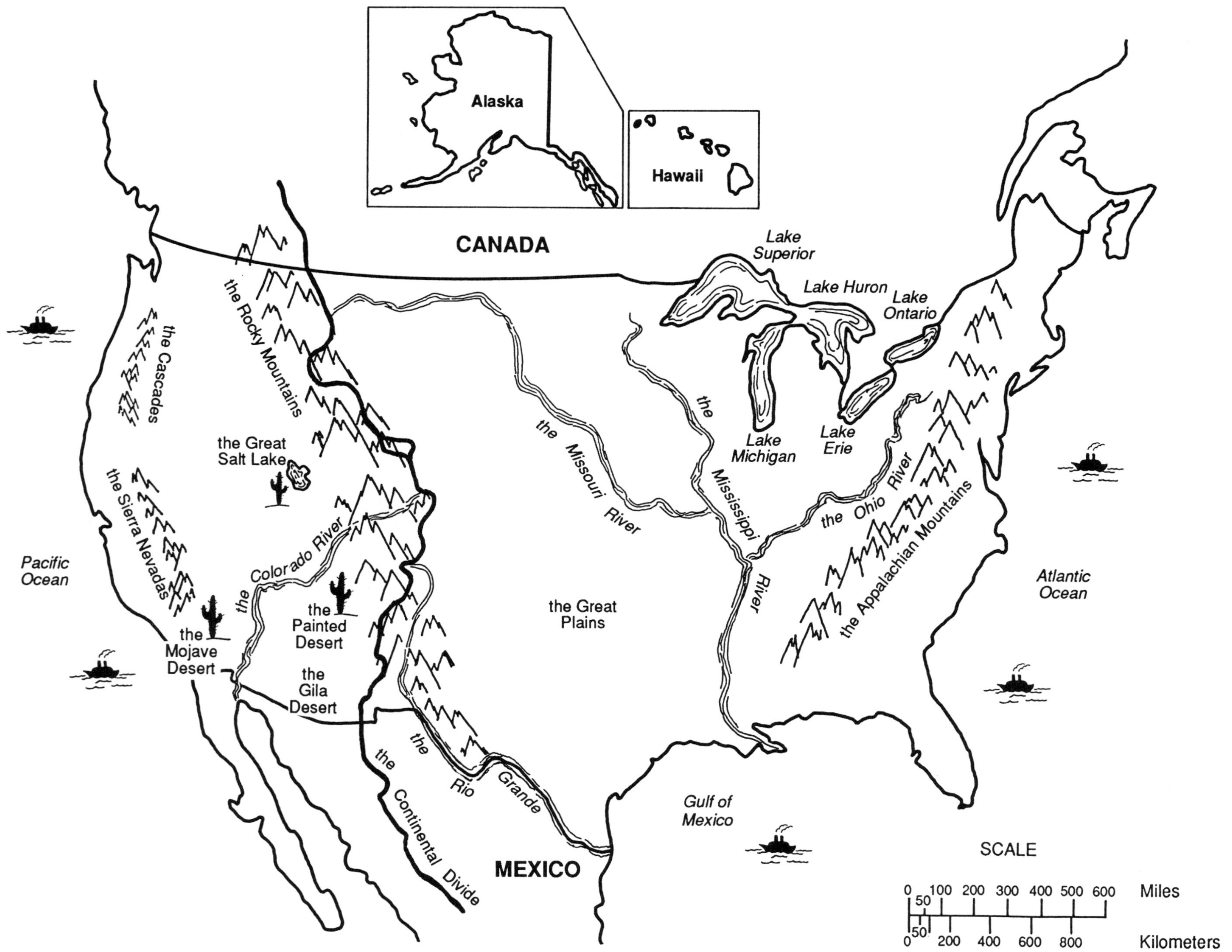
Alaska
Hawaii
CANADA
Lake Superior
Lake Huron
Lake Ontario
Lake Erie
Lake Michigan
the Rocky Mountains
the Cascades
the Great Salt Lake
the Sierra Nevadas
Pacific Ocean
the Colorado River
the Mojave Desert
the Painted Desert
the Gila Desert
the Missouri River
the Mississippi River
the Ohio River
the Appalachian Mountains
the Great Plains
Atlantic Ocean
the Rio Grande
the Continental Divide
MEXICO
Gulf of Mexico
SCALE
0 50 100 200 300 400 500 600   Miles
0 50 200 400 600 800   Kilometers

C   Write T for true and F for false. Correct the false sentences.

1. __F__ In land area, the United States is the ~~largest~~ *fourth* country in the world.

2. ___ All the states except Hawaii and Alaska are together on the North American continent between the Atlantic and Pacific Oceans.

3. ___ It is farther from the Canadian border to the Mexican border than from the east coast to the west coast.

4. ___ The two main mountain ranges in the United States are the Hurons and the Eries.

5. ___ Between the mountain chains are the Great Plains, and there is also a low plain along the Atlantic Ocean.

6. ___ The longest river in the United States is the Gulf of Mexico.

7. ___ The rivers west of the Rockies flow into the Pacific Ocean, and the rivers east of the Rockies flow east.

8. ___ The five Great Lakes are in the southwestern part of the country.

9. ___ The Mojave Desert is west of the Mississippi River.

10. ___ The Great Salt Lake is south of the Sierra Nevada and Cascade Mountains.

D   Use the Scale of Miles on the map. Write the shortest distances between:

1. the Atlantic Ocean and the Pacific Ocean: _______________________________

2. the Canadian and the Mexican borders: _______________________________

3. the Appalachian and the Rocky Mountains: _______________________________

4. The Rocky Mountains and the Sierra Nevada: _______________________________

5. The Mississippi and the Colorado Rivers: _______________________________

6. Lake Michigan and the Gulf of Mexico: _______________________________

7. The Great Salt Lake and the Rio Grande: _______________________________

8. The Mojave and the Gila Deserts: _______________________________

E   Write the letters from the map on the lines.

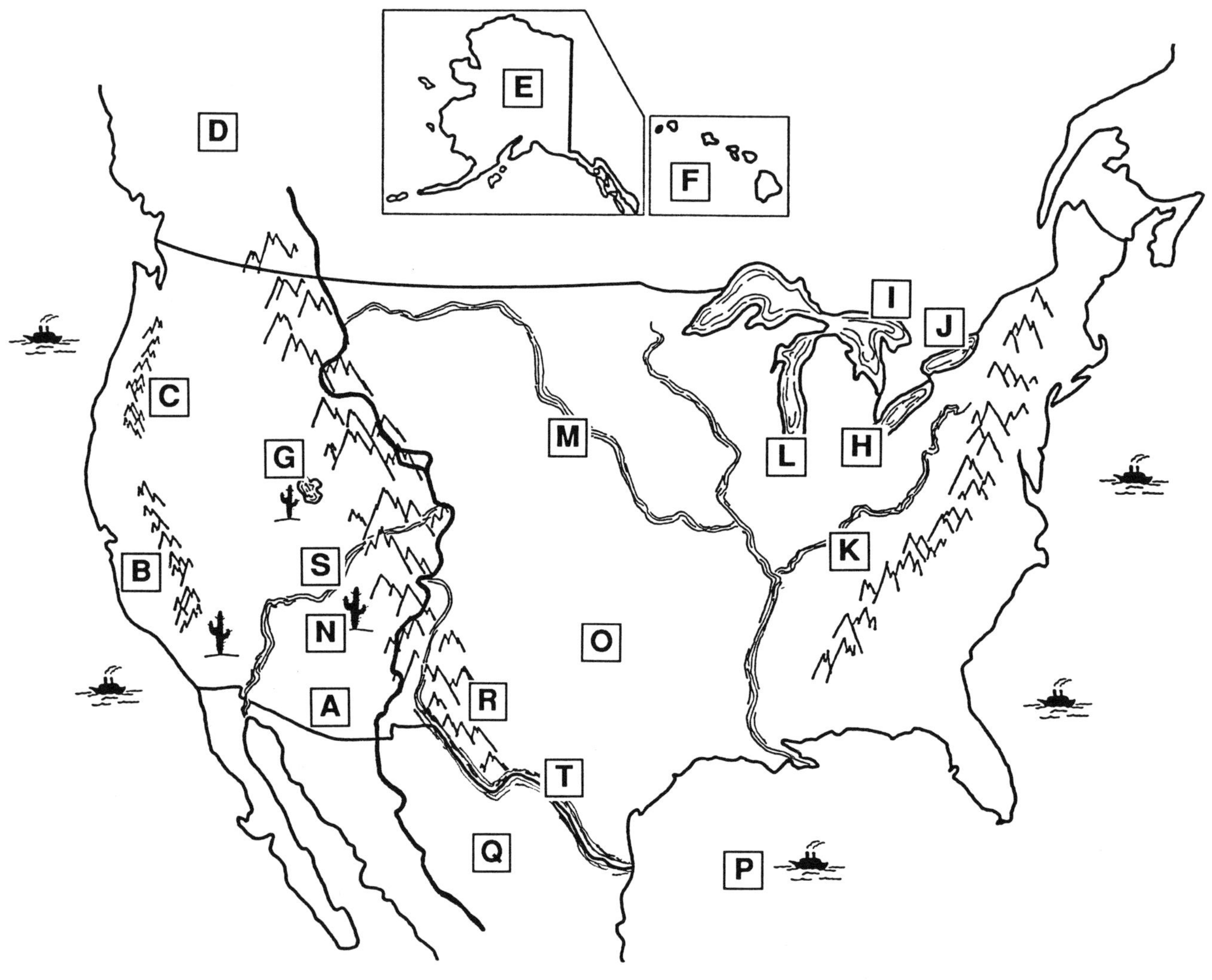

<table>
<tr><td>1.</td><td>_D_</td><td>Canada</td><td>11.</td><td>___</td><td>the Cascade Mountains</td></tr>
<tr><td>2.</td><td>___</td><td>Mexico</td><td>12.</td><td>___</td><td>the Sierra Nevada</td></tr>
<tr><td>3.</td><td>___</td><td>Alaska</td><td>13.</td><td>___</td><td>the Great Plains</td></tr>
<tr><td>4.</td><td>___</td><td>the Hawaiian Islands</td><td>14.</td><td>___</td><td>Lake Huron</td></tr>
<tr><td>5.</td><td>___</td><td>the Gulf of Mexico</td><td>15.</td><td>___</td><td>Lake Erie</td></tr>
<tr><td>6.</td><td>___</td><td>the Ohio River</td><td>16.</td><td>___</td><td>Lake Ontario</td></tr>
<tr><td>7.</td><td>___</td><td>the Missouri River</td><td>17.</td><td>___</td><td>Lake Michigan</td></tr>
<tr><td>8.</td><td>___</td><td>the Colorado River</td><td>18.</td><td>___</td><td>the Great Salt Lake</td></tr>
<tr><td>9.</td><td>___</td><td>the Rio Grande</td><td>19.</td><td>___</td><td>the Painted Desert</td></tr>
<tr><td>10.</td><td>___</td><td>the Rocky Mountains</td><td>20.</td><td>___</td><td>the Gila Desert</td></tr>
</table>

Module 4B: Famous Places

A Washington, D.C.

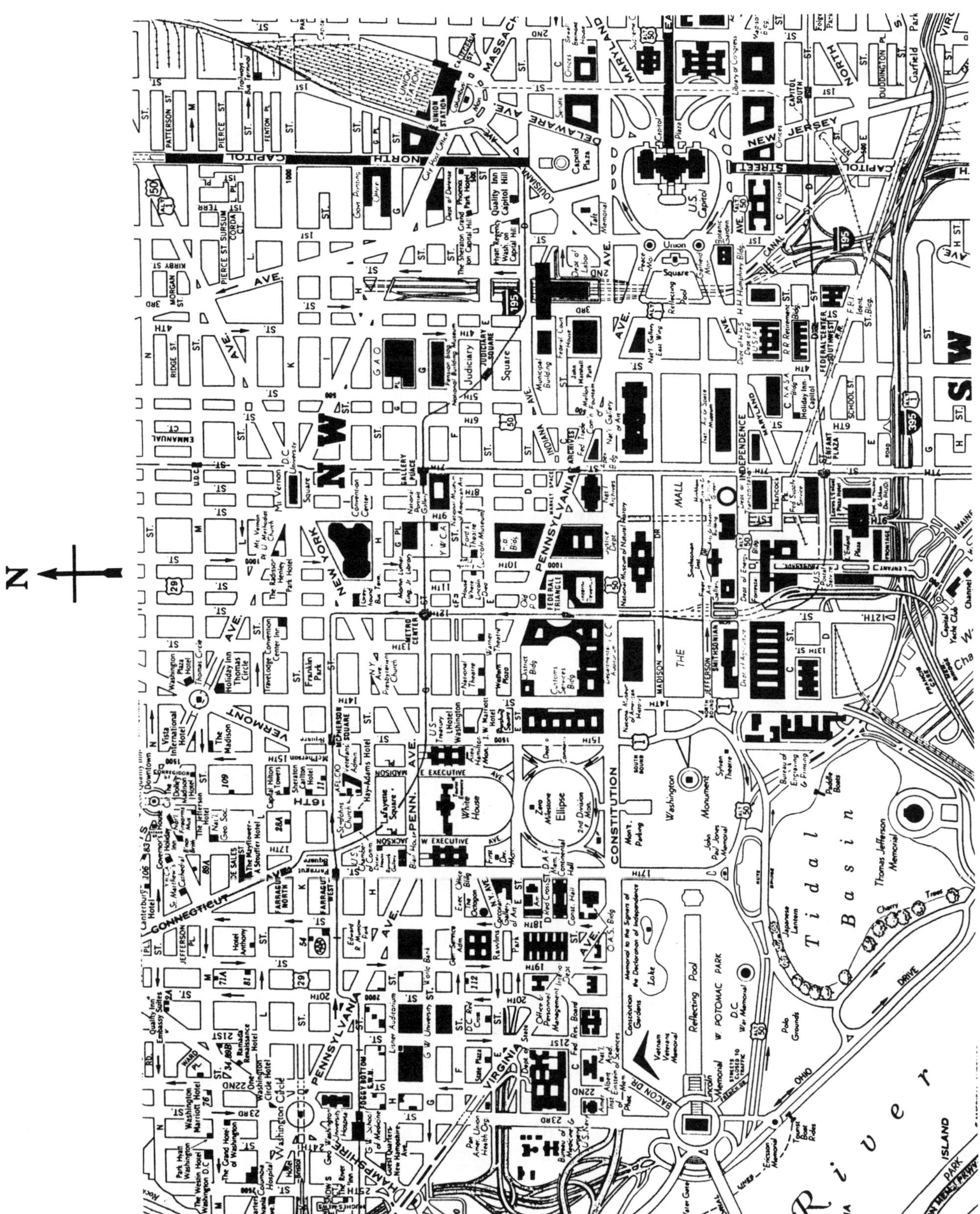

 **Read the story and draw a line on the map on the previous page. Show the sightseeing tour of the writer.**

1. 

    I spent a day in Washington, D.C., the capital city of the United States. We began our sightseeing tour at the U.S. Capitol. Congress--the Senate and the House of Representatives--meets in this building and makes the laws of the land.

2. 

    We walked east from the Capitol to the Library of Congress. This huge library has copies of all books with a U.S. Copyright. Then we crossed East Capitol Street to the Supreme Court. The highest court of the land meets here.

3. 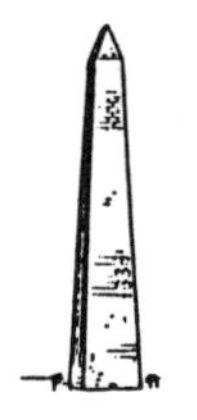

    Next we walked west on Constitution Avenue. In the National Archives we saw two important original documents—the Declaration of Independence and the U.S. Constitution.

4. 

    We continued west to the Washington Monument. This high building was built between 1848 and 1885 in honor of George Washington, the first President of the United States.

5. 

    After that we visited the Jefferson Memorial. This monument was built between 1938 and 1943 in memory of Thomas Jefferson, the third President of the United States. Jefferson wrote the Declaration of Independence.

6. 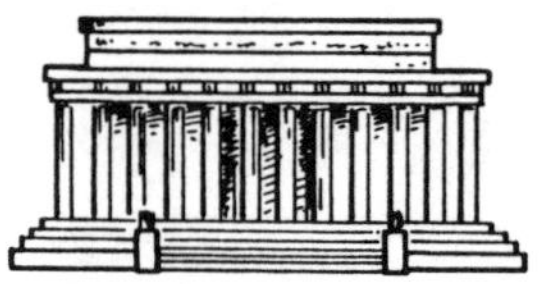

    After the Jefferson Memorial, we saw the Lincoln Memorial. This monument was built in honor of Abraham Lincoln, President during the Civil War. Inside the building are a statue of Lincoln and two murals (wall painting) with symbols of freedom and justice. On two huge stone tablets we read some of Lincoln's important speeches.

7. 

    Finally we went east on Constitution Avenue to the White House at 1600 Pennsylvania Avenue. The White House is the official home of the President.

C Write **T** for true and **F** for false. Correct the false sentences.

1. ___ The Senate and the House of Representatives make the laws of the United States.

2. ___ Congress meets in the White House in New York City.

3. ___ The Library of Congress has only government books.

4. ___ The highest court of the United States is the Supreme Court.

5. ___ In the National Archives on Constitution Avenue you can see the Liberty Bell and murals about Abraham Lincoln.

6. ___ The Washington Monument was built in honor of the President of the United States during the Civil War.

7. ___ Thomas Jefferson, the third President, wrote the Declaration of Independence.

8. ___ In the Lincoln Memorial there are a statue, two murals, and two stone tablets with Lincoln's speeches.

9. ___ The White House on Capitol Street is the official home of the Senators and Representatives.

D In pairs or small groups, use the map to plan your own sightseeing tour of Washington, D.C. List the places to visit in order and tell the class the reasons for your choices.

E Other Famous Places: Match these sentences with the pictures of places on the map on the next page. Write the letters on the lines.

1. ___ New York City has many tourist attractions. You can see the Statue of Liberty, the symbol of freedom for immigrants to the United States. You can visit the Empire State Building, the United Nations Headquarters, Grand Central Station, Central Park, and other famous places.

2. ___ The Gateway Arch is on the Mississippi River in St. Louis, Missouri. It is the symbol of the gateway to the western part of the United States.

3. ___   At Niagara Falls, the waters of Lake Erie fall into Lake Ontario. This tourist attraction is on the border between New York State and Canada.

4. ___   An artist carved the faces of four Presidents in the Black Hills of South Dakota. At Mount Rushmore, you can see huge rock sculptures of George Washington, Thomas Jefferson, Theodore Roosevelt, and Abraham Lincoln.

5. ___   At Yellowstone National Park in Wyoming, you can see some of the natural wonders of North America. Water under the earth turns to steam. It comes to the surface in hot springs or erupts in spectacular geysers.

6. ___   The famous Grand Canyon of the Colorado River is in Arizona. You can explore the spectacular canyon by mule, on foot, or by boat.

7. ___   The Navajo people (native Americans) own the land of Monument Valley on the Arizona-Utah border. The beautiful, natural red rock formations are spectacular monuments of the West.

8. ___   The huge California redwood trees and the giant sequoias of the Sierra Nevada Mountains are some other natural wonders.

9. ___   There are many tourist attractions in San Francisco, California. The Golden Gate Bridge crosses San Francisco Bay.

F   **In pairs or small groups, use the map to plan your own sightseeing tour of the United States. List the places to visit in order and tell the class the reasons for your choices.**

Module 4C: States and Cities: The West

A **Work with a partner. Look only at this map. Your partner will look only at the map on the next page. Take turns asking and answering questions.**

1. Ask about the locations of these states. Listen to your partner's answers and write the names of the states on the map.

| California | Idaho | Montana | Oklahoma | North Dakota |
| Washington | Arizona | Colorado | Nebraska | Hawaii |

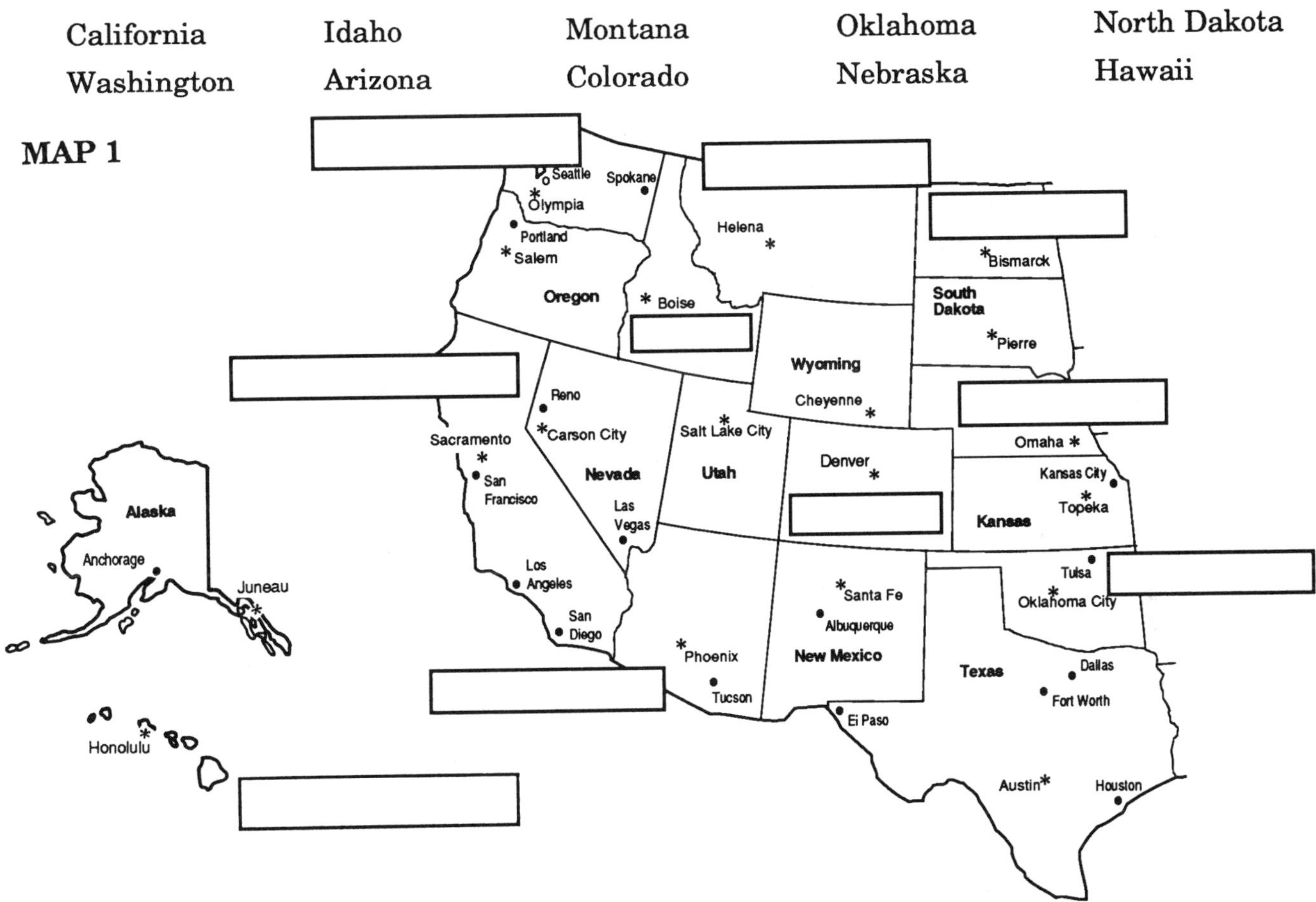

2. Answer your partner's questions about the locations of the states. You can use these sentence patterns:

(Name of state) is

north	northeast
south	northwest
east	southeast
west	southwest

of (name of state).

It's between (name of state) and (name of state).

A **Work with a partner. Look only at this map. Your partner will look only at the map on the previous page. Take turns asking and answering questions.**

1. Ask about the locations of these states. Listen to your partner's answers and write the names of the states on the map.

Oregon   Utah   New Mexico   Wyoming   Alaska

Nevada   Texas   South Dakota   Kansas

MAP 2

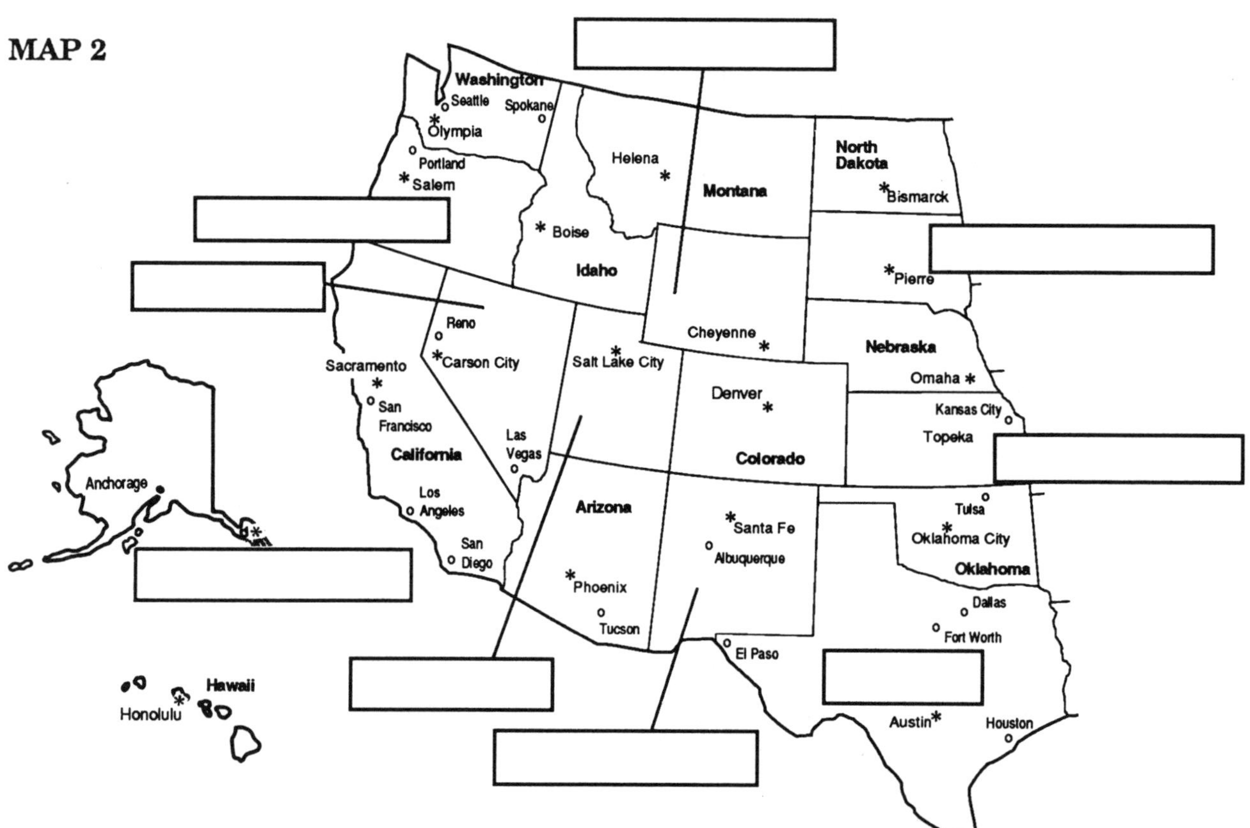

2. Answer your partner's questions about the locations of the states. You can use these sentence patterns:

(Name of state) is	north	northeast	of (name of state).
	south	northwest	
	east	southeast	
	west	southwest	

It's between (name of state) and (name of state).

B Do you know these states from their shapes and cities? Write the letters on the lines.

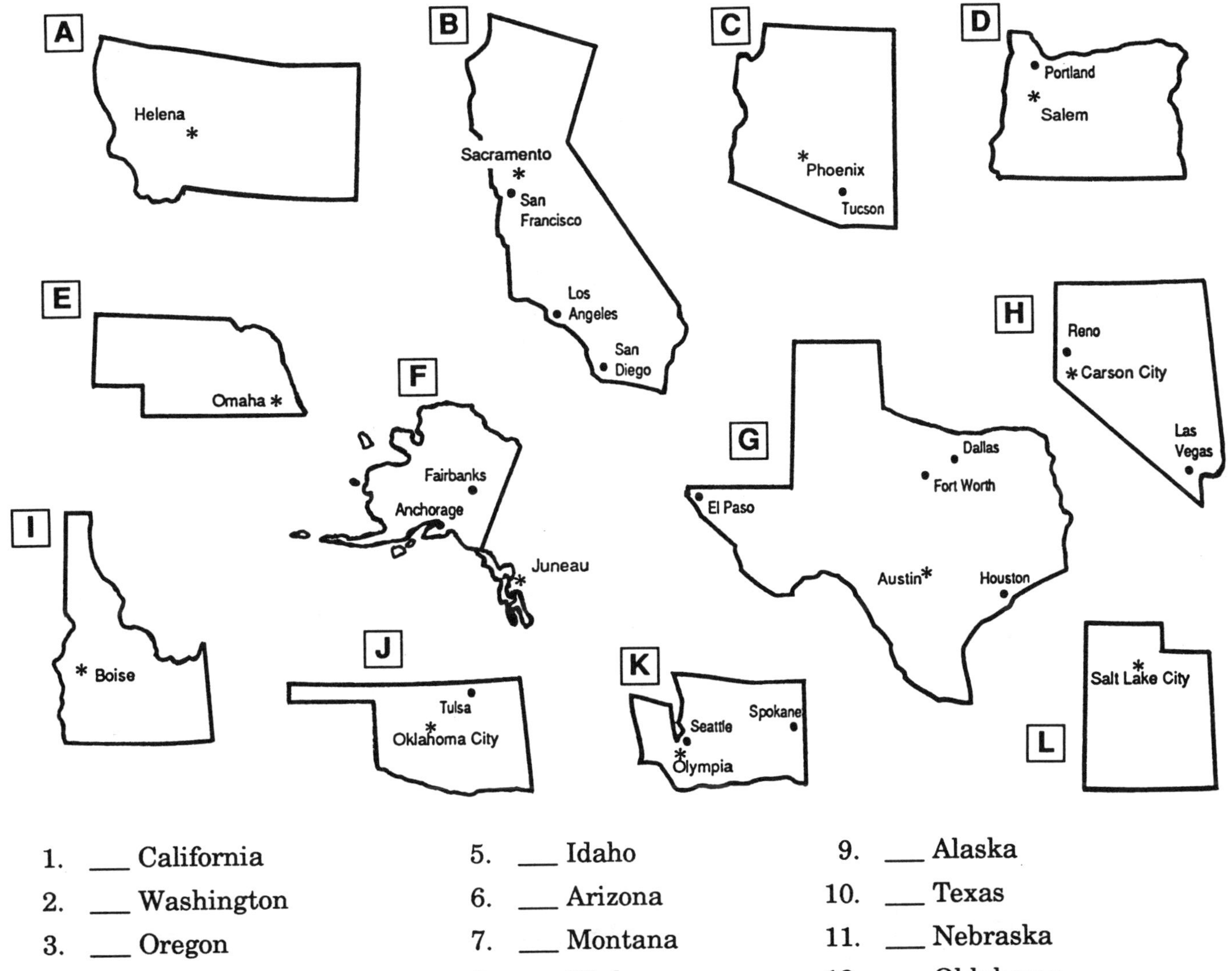

1. ___ California
2. ___ Washington
3. ___ Oregon
4. ___ Nevada

5. ___ Idaho
6. ___ Arizona
7. ___ Montana
8. ___ Utah

9. ___ Alaska
10. ___ Texas
11. ___ Nebraska
12. ___ Oklahoma

C Work in pairs or groups. Make sentences with these sentence patterns about the map of the United States. Your classmates will answer "true" or "false."

(Name of city) is	a city the capital city	in of	the state of (name of state).

EXAMPLES: Student 1: Tucson is a city in the state of Arizona.
Student 2: True.
Student 1: Los Angeles is the capital of California.
Student 2: False. Sacramento is the capital city of California.

 **Facts about the states.**

State	Rank in Land Area (out of 50 states)	Rank in Population (1979 figures)	State	Rank in Land Area (out of 50 states)	Rank in Population (1979 figures)
Alaska	1	50	New Mexico	5	37
Arizona	6	32	North Dakota	17	45
California	3	1	Oklahoma	18	27
Colorado	8	28	Oregon	10	30
Hawaii	47	40	South Dakota	16	44
Idaho	13	41	Texas	2	3
Kansas	14	31	Utah	11	36
Montana	4	43	Washington	20	22
Nebraska	15	35	Wyoming	9	49
Nevada	7	46			

 **Work in pairs or groups. Make sentences with these patterns about the information in D. Your classmates will answer "true" or "false."**

(Name of state) is	bigger / smaller	in	land area / population	than (name of state).

F **Write T for true and F for false. Correct the false sentences.**

1. ___ In general, the states in the western part of the United States are smaller than the states in the East.

2. ___ There are fewer states in the West, but they cover more land area than the states in the East.

3. ___ In general, fewer people live in the eastern states than in the western states.

4. ___ The biggest states in area and in population are in the eastern part of the United States.

Module 4D: States and Cities: The East

A Work with a partner. Look only at this map. Your partner will look only at the map on the next page. Take turns asking and answering questions.

1. Ask about the locations of these states. Listen to your partner's answers and write the names of the states on the map.

> EXAMPLE: Student 1: Where is Georgia, please?
>
> Student 2: Georgia is southeast of Tennessee. It's between Alabama and South Carolina.

MAP 1

Georgia

North Carolina

Delaware

Pennsylvania

Connecticut

Vermont

Kentucky

Indiana

Minnesota

Missouri

Arkansas

Mississippi

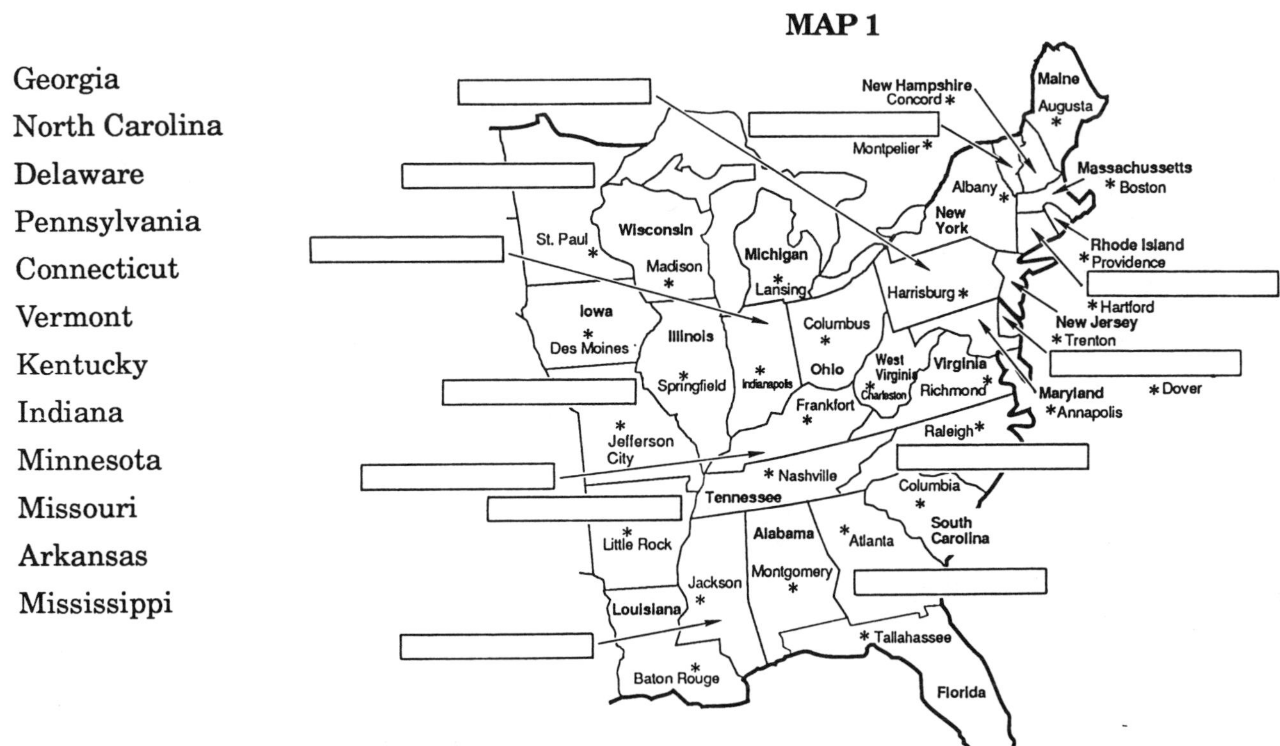

2. Answer your partner's questions about the locations of the states. You can use these sentence patterns:

(Name of state) is	north	northeast	of (name of state).
	south	northwest	
	east	southeast	
	west	southwest	

It's between (name of state) and (name of state).

A **Work with a partner. Look only at this map. Your partner will look only at the map on the previous page. Take turns asking and answering questions.**

1. Ask about the locations of these states. Listen to your partner's answers and write the names of the states on the map.

> EXAMPLE: Student 1:   Where is Georgia, please?
>
> Student 2:   Georgia is southeast of Tennessee. It's between Alabama and South Carolina.

MAP 2

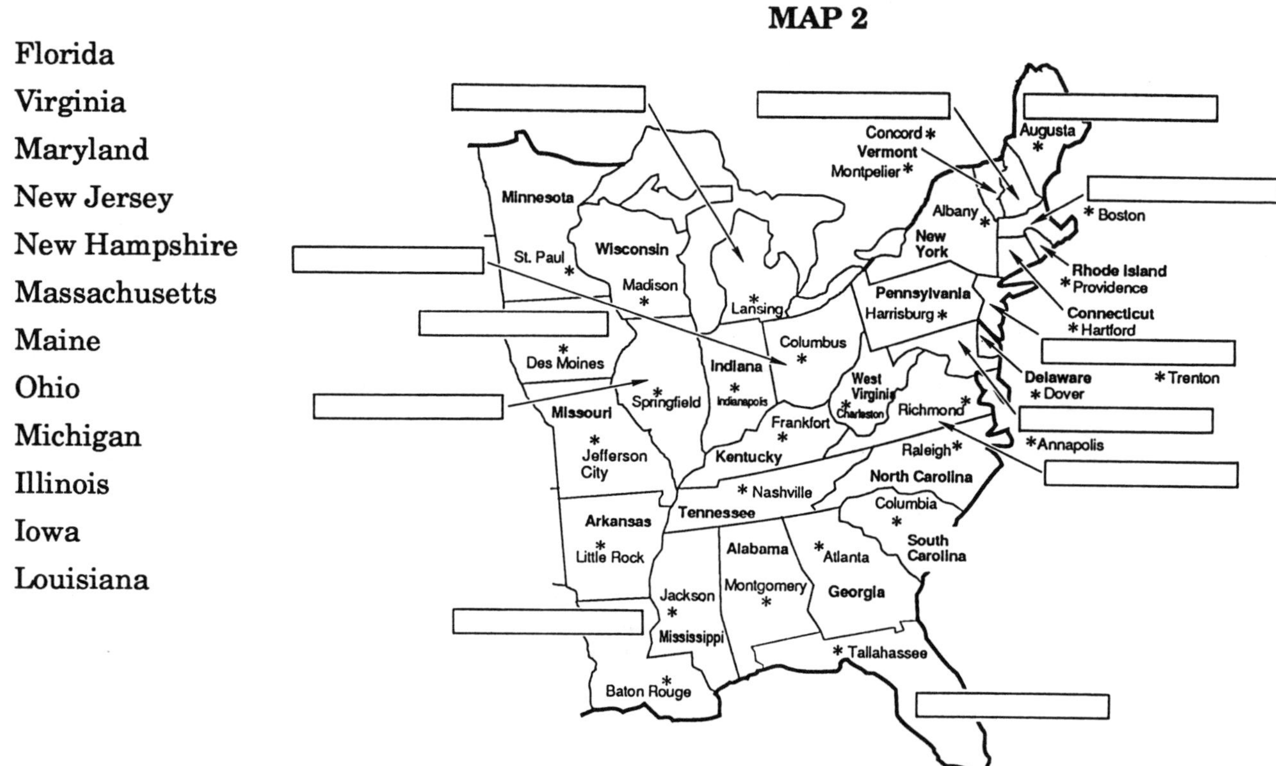

2. Answer your partner's questions about the locations of the states. You can use these sentence patterns:

(Name of state) is	north	northeast	of (name of state).
	south	northwest	
	east	southeast	
	west	southwest	

It's between (name of state) and (name of state).

B **Do you know these states from their shapes and cities? Write the letters on the lines.**

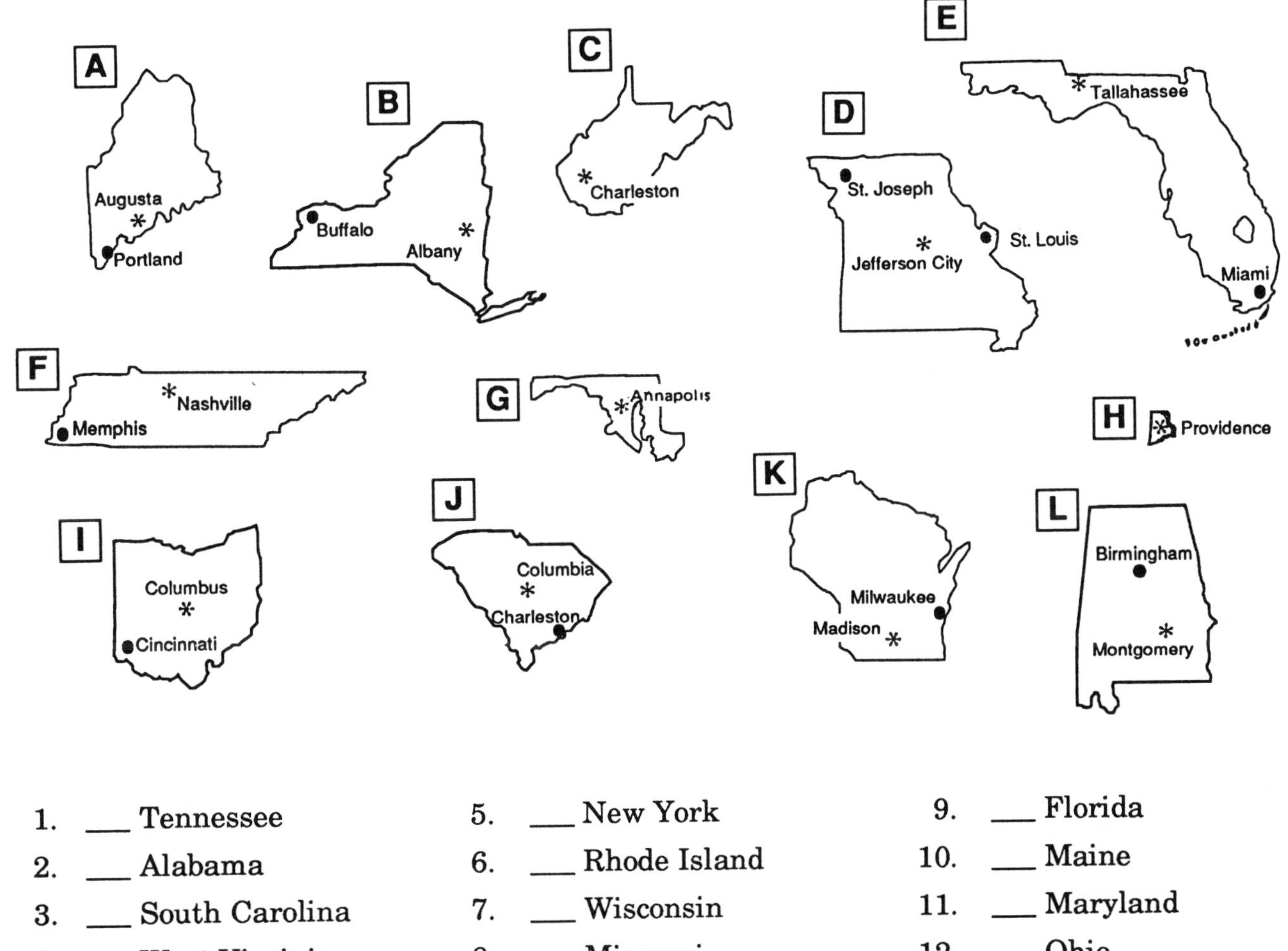

1. ___ Tennessee
2. ___ Alabama
3. ___ South Carolina
4. ___ West Virginia

5. ___ New York
6. ___ Rhode Island
7. ___ Wisconsin
8. ___ Missouri

9. ___ Florida
10. ___ Maine
11. ___ Maryland
12. ___ Ohio

C **Work in pairs or groups. Make sentences with these sentence patterns about the map of the United States. Your classmates will answer "true" or "false."**

(Name of city) is	a city the capital city	in of	the state of (name of state).

EXAMPLES: Student 1: Memphis is a city in the state of Tennessee.
Student 2: True.
Student 1: New York City is the capital of New York.
Student 2: False. Albany is the capital city of New York.

D Facts about the states.

State	Rank in Land Area (out of 50 states)	Rank in Population (1979 figures)	State	Rank in Land Area (out of 50 states)	Rank in Population (1979 figures)
Alabama	29	21	Mississippi	32	29
Arkansas	27	33	Missouri	19	15
Connecticut	48	24	New Hampshire	44	42
Delaware	49	47	New Jersey	46	9
Florida	22	8	New York	30	2
Georgia	21	14	North Carolina	28	11
Illinois	24	5	Ohio	35	6
Indiana	38	12	Pennsylvania	33	4
Iowa	25	26	Rhode Island	50	39
Kentucky	37	23	South Carolina	40	25
Louisiana	31	20	Tennessee	34	17
Maine	39	38	Vermont	43	48
Maryland	42	18	Virginia	36	13
Massachusetts	45	10	West Virginia	41	34
Michigan	23	7	Wisconsin	26	16
Minnesota	12	19			

E Work in pairs or groups. Make sentences with these patterns about the information in D. Your classmates will answer "true" or "false."

(Name of state) is | bigger / smaller | in | land area / population | than (name of state).

F Play the game of "Geography." The first player names a place (city, state, river, etc.) in the United States. The second player names a place that begins with the last letter of the first place. The next player names a place that begins with the last letter of the second place, and so on.

EXAMPLES:　Student 1: Vermont (ends with t)
　　　　　　Student 2: Tennessee (begins with t, ends with e)
　　　　　　Student 3: Erie (Lake)

You might want to play this game in teams. You can use maps of the United States for ideas.

Citizenship

Module 5A: Becoming a Citizen

A Eligibility Requirements

Before you can become a naturalized citizen of the United States, you must usually meet certain requirements.

1. You must be at least eighteen years old.

2. You must live in the United States as a legal resident for at least five years before you apply for citizenship. You can't leave the country for more than one year continuously or for more than thirty months in total.

3. You must be "of good moral character" and loyal to the United States. For example, you can't be a criminal or an alcoholic. You can't lie under oath or refuse to serve in the U.S. armed forces. You can't be a member of the Communist Party.

4. If you are under fifty years old and haven't lived in the United States for at least twenty years, you must be able to read, write, speak, and understand basic English. At the citizenship interview, you'll have to answer some questions in simple English about U.S. government and history.*

B Write T for true and F for false. Correct the false sentences.

To be eligible for citizenship, you must meet these requirements.

1. ___ You must be under eighteen years old.

2. ___ You must live in the United States for at least fifteen years before you apply.

3. ___ You can't leave the United States for five years before you apply.

4. ___ You must be "of good moral character" and loyal to the United States.

5. ___ You must read, write, speak, and understand English perfectly if you are under fifty years old.

6. ___ You must learn something about U.S. government and history.

*Much of the information in this book is based on information in the Federal citizenship texts–*United States History: 1600-1987, U.S. Government Structure,* and *Citizenship Education and Naturalization Information,* Immigration and Naturalization Service, U.S. Department of Justice, 1987. The questions in the oral citizenship examination are based on information and questions in the Federal texts. Also, you can get more specific information on the requirements for citizenship and the exceptions from these books and the INS.

 **In pairs, roleplay an INS interview. (If you are a U.S. citizen, you can play the role of the interviewer or of an immigrant.)**

| Do you...? | Are you...? | Have you...? | Can you...? |

EXAMPLES: Student 1: Do you want to become a U.S. citizen?
Student 2: Yes, I do.
Student 1: Are you at least eighteen years old?
Student 2: Yes, I am.

yes   no

1. ... want to become a U.S. citizen? ☐ ☐
2. ... at least eighteen years old? ☐ ☐
3. ... lived in the United States as a permanent immigrant for at least five years? ☐ ☐
4. ... qualify for legalization (if you are not a permanent immigrant now)? ☐ ☐
5. ... left the country for more than one year continuously in the last five years? ☐ ☐
6. ... lived outside the country for more than thirty months in the last five years? ☐ ☐
7. ... of good moral character and loyal to the United States? ☐ ☐
8. ... a criminal or an alcoholic? ☐ ☐
9. ... lied under oath about your eligibility for citizenship under the immigration and naturalization laws? ☐ ☐
10. ... refused to serve in the U.S. armed forces? ☐ ☐
11. ... a member of the Communist Party? ☐ ☐
12. ... a member of any organization in favor of violence against the U.S. government? ☐ ☐
13. ... read and write basic English? ☐ ☐
14. ... speak and understand basic English? ☐ ☐
15. ... answer questions in simple English about U.S. government and history? ☐ ☐

 **In small groups, discuss the answers to these questions.**

1. To be eligible for U.S. citizenship, how must you be able to answer the questions in C?

2. Is your partner eligible for citizenship now? Why or why not?

E Steps to Citizenship

1. 

   Get an application package from the Immigration and Naturalization Service. Fill out the personal information on the application form, the biographic information sheet, and the fingerprint chart. You can get fingerprinted at a police station, sheriff's office, or some INS offices.

2. 

   Read the requirements carefully. You may need other documents, such as an alien registration receipt and card, a selective service registration, a passport or other record of entry to the United States, or a marriage certificate. Send them with the application forms and three unsigned photographs of your face to the INS.

3. 

   The INS will schedule an interview for you. At the interview you will have to answer some oral questions about U.S. government and history. Then you will probably have to take a simple dictation test and sign your name. If you pass, you can file a petition for naturalization and pay a fee.

4. 

   Your final hearing is in court before a judge. To become a citizen, you must take an oath of allegiance to the United States. Then you will receive a certificate of naturalization.

Here is the oath of allegiance (promise of loyalty):

"I hereby declare, on oath, that I absolutely and entirely renounce and abjure all allegiance and fidelity to any foreign prince, potentate, state, or sovereignty of whom or which I have heretofore been a subject or citizen; that I will support and defend the Constitution and laws of the United States of America against all enemies, foreign and domestic; that I will bear true faith and allegiance to the same; that I will bear arms on behalf of the United States when required by law; that I will perform noncombatant service in the Armed Forces of the United States when required by the law; that I will perform work of national importance under civilian direction when required by the law; and that I take this obligation freely without any mental reservation or purpose of evasion; so help me God. In acknowledgment whereof I have hereunto affixed my signature."

 **Check (✓) the necessary and possible things to send to the INS to apply for citizenship.**

1. ✓ the application form, biographic information sheet, and fingerprint chart.
2. ___ a photograph of the police station or sheriff's office.
3. ___ your alien registration receipt card
4. ___ your selective service registration
5. ___ your work records and letters from your employers
6. ___ your passport or record of entry to the United States
7. ___ an American flag and a copy of the Pledge of Allegiance
8. ___ your marriage certificate
9. ___ three unsigned photographs of your face
10. ___ your U.S. government and history tests and a dictation paper from school

G **Number the things to do to apply for citizenship 1–8 in time order.**

___ Go to your scheduled interview, answer some oral questions about U.S. government and history, and take a dictation test.

___ Fill out the personal information in the application package from the INS.

___ Get fingerprinted at a police station, sheriff's office, or INS office.

___ Take the oath of allegiance to the United States.

___ File a petition for naturalization and pay a fee.

___ Receive your certificate of naturalization.

___ Send the forms from the application package with other necessary documents and three photographs to the INS.

___ Go to a court hearing before a judge.

 **In your own words, tell the necessary steps to apply for citizenship.**

Module 5B: The Duties of Citizens

A Do you know your responsibilities as a citizen? In pairs or small groups, discuss these sentences. Write a, b, or c on each line. Then check your answers on the next page.

a = things you must do
b = things you should or may do
c = things you mustn't or shouldn't do

1. **C** Oppose the Constitution of the United States.

2. **a** Protect your own rights and respect the rights of others.

3. ___ Obey the laws of your nation, state, county, and city.

4. ___ If you disagree with a policy or law, write your representative or senator to try to change it.

5. ___ Serve in the U.S. Army, Navy, Marines, or Air Force if there is a draft (men only).

6. ___ Join the armed forces in peacetime.

7. ___ Serve on a jury if the court calls you and you are not excused.

8. ___ Stop work temporarily to do jury duty.

9. ___ Pay income taxes on time or pay the penalties.

10. ___ Refuse to report all your income so that your tax bill will be lower.

11. ___ Register to vote.

12. ___ Learn about the candidates (people running for office) and issues (topics of discussion) before every election.

13. ___ Discriminate against women, blacks, or members of national groups.

14. ___ Attend community or public meetings.

15. ___ Stay away from your children's school and refuse to help them with their homework.

16. ___ Volunteer (work without pay) in the community.

17. ___ Speak only your native language.

18. ___ Take English classes at a local college or adult school.

B **In groups, tell the duties and responsibilities of U.S. citizens. You can use this sentence pattern.**

| As a citizen, you | have to
mustn't
ought to
shouldn't | ___________________________. |

C **Which sentences do you agree with? Check them. Then in groups, choose one sentence and talk about it for one minute. Your classmates will agree or disagree and tell the reasons for their opinions.**

1. ___ If you don't agree with a law, it is your responsibility to try to change it.

2. ___ There should be no military draft, and only volunteers should serve in the armed forces.

3. ___ Everyone should serve on a jury even if it is difficult to leave work and take the time for jury duty.

4. ___ Everyone cheats on their income tax because it is unfair.

5. ___ You should not try to lower your tax obligation because tax money is necessary to improve your community and the country.

6. ___ If citizens don't vote, the system of the U.S. can't be truly democratic.

7. ___ You can make an important difference in your community if you attend public meetings.

8. ___ Discrimination is against the law because members of all races, religions, and nationalities are equal.

9. ___ You should join the PTA (Parent-Teachers Association) at your children's school.

10. ___ You can volunteer to help at a hospital, church, school, or community organization even if your English is not very good.

11. ___ It is important for all citizens and residents of the U.S. to know English well.

12. ___ You can learn English better if you get involved in community activities.

Answers to Exercise A

1. c 2. a 3. a 4. b 5. a 6. b 7. a 8. a 9. a 10. c 11. b 12. b 13. c 14. b 15. c 16. b 17. c 18. b

 **Walk around the classroom and ask your classmates these questions. When someone answers *yes*, write his or her name. Then ask questions about the experience and write notes on the answers.**

Have you ever...

1.   ...served in the armed forces?

2.   ...served on a jury?

3.   ...had a problem with the Internal Revenue Service (the IRS)?

4.   ...run for office or helped a political candidate?

5.   ...attended a public meeting?

6.   ...written to a public official about your opinion on a law?

7.   ...experienced discrimination because of race, religion, or nationality?

8.   ...been involved in an activity or organization at your children's school?

9.   ...volunteered to help at a hospital, church, or community organization?

10.   ...tried to improve your English through community involvement?

 **Tell the class about one classmate's experience.**

 **Citizens and residents of the U.S. sometimes write their opinions in "Letters to the Editor." These appear in local newspapers, and other readers may write answers. In small groups, discuss these "Letters to the Editor" and write answers to them.**

1.

Dear Editor:

Many states are changing their laws, even their constitutions, to make English the official state language. Why do they want these "English only" laws? People use English all over America! Of course, everybody should learn English, but I'm afraid that these new laws will discriminate against me and my people. My native language is important to me. I want to use it when I pray and when I have meetings with friends from "the old country." I also put bilingual signs in my store, and I want my children to continue to get bilingual help in school. I know my English will never be good enough to understand voting or tax documents, so I want the government to continue to prepare these papers in two languages. I believe that a great nation should have plenty of room for different cultures and languages.

2.

Dear Editor:

Why should I pay my taxes honestly? My neighbor makes dresses, and she doesn't pay tax on her earnings from them. I am a waitress and I don't want to report my tips. What does the government do with all that tax money? The city hasn't repaired our street. Gangs, not the police, are controlling our neighborhood. There are not enough teachers in my daughter's school. After I pay my tax bill each year, I have no money left to buy health insurance. When my daughter broke her arm last year, my husband and I had to spend $3000 of our own money because the government didn't give us any help.

 **In your local newspaper, find a letter of interest about a national, state, or local issue. Read and discuss it as a class. You might want to write an answer together and send it to the newspaper.**

Module 5C: Voting

Work in groups. Discuss these questions about elections in the U.S. Decide on the answers and then check them on page 64.

1. What are the primaries?
   a. the first general elections of new states
   b. party elections in individual states

2. Who do voters choose in a closed primary election?
   a. Presidential and Vice Presidential candidates of their own political party
   b. the mayor, city council members, sheriff, and district attorney

3. What happens at the national convention of a political party?
   a. Local officials reform the politics of all opposing parties.
   b. Elected delegates nominate candidates for President and Vice President and decide on a party "platform" (political position).

4. How often and when is there a national election?
   a. Congress decides the date of a national election.
   b. every four years on the Tuesday after the first Monday in November

5. How often and when do state and local elections take place?
   a. The dates vary from state to state, but they are often at the same time as national elections.
   b. every two years on February 28 or 29

6. What is the "electoral college" process?
   a. a system of indirect voting for President and Vice President
   b. a group of professors and teachers in political schools

7. How many "electors" does each state get in the electoral college?
   a. The number of electors depends on the size (area) of the state and the date of admission to the Union.
   b. The number of electors for each party is equal to the number of that state's representatives and senators.

8. After citizens vote in a national election, how does the electoral college process work?
   a. The Presidential and Vice Presidential candidates of the party with the highest number of votes in each state win all the electoral votes of that state.
   b. The candidates of each party win electoral votes in proportion to the popular vote (the percentage of votes they have received in the whole country).

9. Can the electoral process be changed?
   a. No, because all the states are satisfied with it.
   b. Yes, but only with a Constitutional amendment.

 **Work in pairs. Look only at this page and ask your partner these questions about voting. Your partner will tell you the answers from the information on the next page. Take notes on the information.**

1. Why should citizens vote?

2. Who can vote?

3. Do I have to take a test or pay to vote?

4. What is the state and local residency requirement for voting?

5. How can I register to vote?

6. Do I have to belong to a political party?

7. How do I get information about the candidates and the issues?

8. Where can I vote?

9. How do I vote?

10. What can I do if I can't get to the polling place?

B **Work in pairs. Look only at this page. To answer your partner's questions about voting, find the information and tell it to your partner. He or she will take notes.**

- All U.S. citizens (both sexes and all races) over the age of eighteen can vote, except criminals and the mentally ill.

- The right to vote is the most important right of U.S. citizens, as well as the most important responsibility. All votes have equal value. If citizens don't vote, the system of democracy can't be truly representative.

- It depends on state law. For example, California requires ninety days' residence in a county and thirty days' residence in a precinct (voting district) before you can vote there.

- No, you don't. No state may give you a literacy (reading and writing) test or charge you a poll (voting) tax before you vote.

- You can get a voter registration form at many public locations, such as post offices and libraries. You can also call the county clerk or Registrar of Voters to get a form. Fill it out and send it in.

- You can inform yourself about the candidates from T.V., radio, newspapers, and advertising mail. You can also get brochures, pamphlets, and newsletters from the headquarters of political parties.

- If you can't get to the polling place, you can get an absentee ballot from the Registrar of Voters.

- The back of your sample ballot (voting booklet) will tell you your polling (voting) place.

- No, you don't. You can register as a party member if you want to, but you can also write "no party" on the voter registration form.

- To vote, go to your polling place, give the volunteers there your name and address, and get a ballot. All voting is secret. Read the instructions carefully to vote.

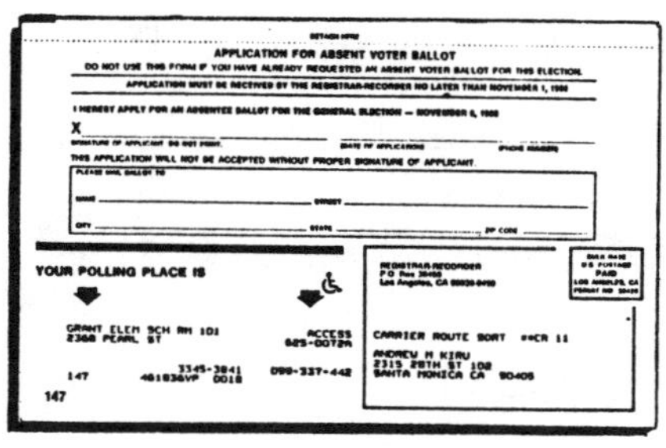

 **Answer the questions with information from these ballot parts.**

DEMOCRATIC
PRESIDENT OF THE UNITED STATES

PRESIDENTIAL PREFERENCE Vote for One	AL GORE	Democratic	2 ➡ ◯
	PAUL SIMON	Democratic	3 ➡ ◯
	JESSE JACKSON	Democratic	4 ➡ ◯
	LYNDON LAROUCHE	Democratic	5 ➡ ◯
	MICHAEL S. DUKAKIS	Democratic	6 ➡ ●

1. What kind of election (primary or general) was this ballot for? _______________________

    For which party? ____

2. Who did the voter vote for? ____

Vote for One Party	MICHAEL S. DUKAKIS, for President LLOYD BENTSEN, for Vice President	Democratic	2 ➡ ◯
	RON PAUL, for President ANDRE V. MARROU, for Vice President	Libertarian	4 ➡ ◯
	LENORA B. FULANI, for President B. KWAKU DUREN, for Vice President	Independent	6 ➡ ◯
	JAMES C. GRIFFIN, for President CHARLES J. MORSA, for Vice President	American Independent	8 ➡ ◯
	GEORGE BUSH, for President DAN QUAYLE, for Vice President	Republican	10 ➡ ◯

3. What offices were these candidates running for? _______________________________

    ____

4. How many political parties had candidates on the ballot? _______________________

5. Who was the Democratic candidate for President? _______________________________

    For Vice President? ____

6. What party did Ron Paul and Andre V. Marrou belong to? _______________________

7. What year was this election? ___________ Who won? _________________________

Answers to Exercise A:
1. b 2. a 3. b 4. b 5. a 6. a 7. b 8. a 9. b

Module 5D: Election Issues

A   The Power of the People

If enough citizens strongly oppose an elected government official, they can start a movement for a recall (removal from office). First, they have to gather the required number of signatures on a petition. Then they "campaign" to present their views to the people. Finally, the voters decide on the recall issue at an election.

In a similar way, by collecting enough signatures on a petition, citizens can put an initiative (proposed law) on the ballot. The state legislature can also present a ballot measure directly to the voters in the form of a referendum. Occasionally a referendum, such as a protest against an unfair law, comes directly from the people. An initiative or referendum appears on the ballot in the form of a "proposition" or "state measure" and can cover only one issue. It needs a majority of votes to pass.

B   Match the words with their meanings. Write the letters on the lines.

1. ___   an initiative   a. the voting booklet or card

2. ___   a petition   b. usually, a measure presented to the voters by the legislature

3. ___   a recall   c. a state or local measure on the ballot

4. ___   a referendum   d. removal of an official from office

5. ___   the ballot   e. a signed request or demand

6. ___   a proposition   f. a measure begun by action of the people

C   Write T for true and F for false. Correct the false sentences.

1. ___   If a politician wins an election, there is no way for the voters to remove him or her from office.

2. ___   To put a recall or an initiative measure on the ballot, the voters must get the support of all major political parties.

3. ___   Citizens can protest an unfair law through a referendum.

4. ___   A proposition on the ballot needs the approval of all registered voters to pass.

 **An Example of a Ballot Initiative**

The goal of Proposition 99 (state of California, 1988) was to raise the cigarette tax from $ .10 to $ .35 per pack and to add taxes to other tobacco products. Revenue from this tax would go to the following: 45% for medical care to the poor, 20% to help people to stop smoking, 5% to study diseases caused by smoking, 5% to protect wildlife and parkland, and 20% for any of the above programs.

Opponents of Proposition 99 believed that doctors and hospitals would receive most of the tax money, not poor people. They said that the measure would unfairly tax one group of citizens, smokers. They also warned that the tax would cause people to smuggle cigarettes (bring them illegally) from other states.

Supporters said that the 25-cent tax was not high and that smokers should pay the high costs of disease and fire damage causd by cigarettes. They did not believe that an additional cigarette tax would lead to smuggling because the taxes in nearby states were already higher than those in California.

 **List arguments for and against Proposition 99. (You can add opinions of your own.) Then mark your "vote" on the ballot.**

For	Against
1. _tax - not high_	1. __________
2. __________	2. __________
3. __________	3. __________
__________	__________
__________	__________

99 CIGARETTE AND TOBACCO TAX. BENEFIT FUND. INITIATIVE. Imposes additional cigarette and tobacco tax for medical care, health education, other purposes. Fiscal Impact: Raises state revenues of approximately $300 million in 1988–89 (part-year) and $600 million in 1989–90 (first full-year). State administrative costs are estimated at $500,000 in 1988–89 and $300,000 in subsequent years.	159	YES ➡ ◯
	160	NO ➡ ◯

 **An Example of a Referendum**

In 1988, the California legislature presented Proposition 84, a bond referendum, to the people. (A bond is a way for the government to keep borrowed money for a long time. Private buyers purchase the bonds, and the government pays back the money with interest from tax revenues.)

Proposition 84 asked for $300 million in bonds to help solve the problem of the homeless (people without places to live). Here is the measure that appeared on the ballot:

84   **HOUSING AND HOMELESS BOND ACT OF 1988.** This act provides for a bond issue of three hundred million dollars ($300,000,000) to provide funds for a housing program that includes: (1) emergency shelters and transitional housing for homeless families and individuals, (2) new rental housing for families and individuals including rental housing which meets the special needs of the elderly, disabled, and farmworkers, (3) rehabilitation and preservation of older homes and rental housing, and (4) home purchase assistance for first-time homebuyers.

107   **YES ➡ ◯**

109   **NO ➡ ◯**

Supporters of the measure said that it would get homeless people off the streets. It would help many people rent apartments and buy homes. The money would also create jobs and improve the economy.

Opponents of Proposition 84 said that the government should not try to solve the homeless problem with tax money. Instead, it should make it easier to build new housing with more lenient building laws. It should also change city zoning laws to open more space for low-income housing.

G   **Write the words from the ballot measure in F.**

The goals of Proposition 84 were:

to build emergency (1) ____**shelters**____ for (2) ______________ people; to provide new

(3) ________________ housing for people with special needs, such as (4) ______________,

(5) ________________, and farmworkers; to make possible the (6) ________________ and

(7) ________________ of older homes and rental housing; and to help (8) ________________

purchase homes.

 **List arguments for and against Proposition 84. (You can add opinions of your own.) Then mark your "vote" on the ballot in F.**

For

1. _______________________________

2. _______________________________

3. _______________________________

____

____

Against

1. _______________________________

2. _______________________________

3. _______________________________

____

____

 **Election Issues**

Candidates for election should present their opinions on the issues so that citizens can base their voting decisions on those views. Here are some issues from a recent election:

- Should abortion (ending a pregnancy) be legal?

- Should there be public health insurance for all U.S. residents?

- Should tax money go to the development of fuel sources of energy other than coal and oil?

- Should it be illegal to smoke in all public places?

- Should the government test everyone in the U.S. for AIDS?

- Should the government cut down on defense spending to have more money for education, health care, and protection of the environment?

 **Work in groups of six to ten. Choose one of the national issues in I. Then divide your group into two smaller equal groups. One of these smaller groups will list reasons to answer the question *yes*, and the other will list reasons to answer the question *no*.**

Have a "political debate" on the issue for the class. One "speaker" from the "yes" group will tell the class an argument, a student from the "no" group will tell an opposing argument, and so on. Then the class will discuss and vote on the issue.

Repeat the activity with another issue and another group of "debaters."

Module 6A: Overview of the Constitution

A Introduction to the U.S. Constitution

After the Revolutionary War, the Articles of Confederation (1781) were the basis of the new American government. But this weak government did not work very well. The delegates to the Constitutional Convention of 1787 revised the Articles of Confederation. The result was the U.S. Constitution. Three main principles form the basis of the Constitution:

1. the separation of powers of the three branches of government
2. government of, for, and by the people
3. basic human rights (individual freedom, equality, and justice)

The Constitution has three parts:

1. The Preamble tells its purposes: to protect the nation and to assure justice, peace, and liberty for all.
2. The Document contains seven articles.
3. Twenty-six Amendments guarantee individual rights and freedoms and establish other basic principles of government.

B Write the words from A.

1. After the Revolutionary War, _____the Articles of Confederation_____ (1781) were the basis of the new American government.

2. The result of the Constitutional Convention of 1787 was ________________________.

3. One of the main principles of the Constitution is the ________________ of powers of the three ________________ of government.

4. Another principle is government of, for, and by ________________.

5. The third principle is basic ________________, such as individual ________________, equality, and ________________.

6. The three parts of the Constitution are ________________, the seven ________________ of the Document, and the twenty-six ________________.

C The Document

Article One created the Legislative Branch of government. It established these principles, among others:

1. Congress makes the laws of the nation.
2. The two houses of Congress are the Senate and the House of Representatives.
3. The people of each state elect two Senators.
4. The population of each state determines the number of Representatives.

Article Two established the Executive Branch of government, the Presidency. Here are a few of its principles:

1. The Electoral College elects the President.
2. The President is the chief executive of the nation and Commander in Chief of the armed forces.
3. The President has certain powers, such as to enforce laws.
4. The President may initiate the law-making process.

Article Three created the Judicial Branch under these principles:

1. The Supreme Court is the highest court of the land. It is a court of last appeal, and its decisions are final.
2. It is the responsibility of the Supreme Court to defend and interpret the principles of the Constitution.
3. Residents of the U.S. have the right to trial by jury.

Article Four defined the relationship among the states and the relationship of the states to the Federal government. It included these principles:

1. U.S. residents have the same rights in all states.
2. All states have a republican form of government.
3. Congress may admit new states and make laws for U.S. territories.

Article Five described ways to amend (change) the Constitution.

1. Congress may propose (suggest) an amendment if two-thirds of both houses vote for it.
2. The states may initiate an amendment. If two-thirds of all state legislatures agree to propose it, Congress will call a national convention.
3. To add the amendment to the Constitution, three-fourths of the state legislatures or special state conventions must ratify (officially approve) it.

Article Six declared the Constitution the Supreme Law of the Land.

1. No state constitution or law or judge may contradict (state the opposite of) the Constitution.
2. All public officials must promise to support the Constitution in an official oath.

Article Seven declared that nine states must ratify the Constitution for it to become law.

D **In the parentheses, write the number of the Article of the Constitution that contains the answer to each question. Then write the answer in a few words on the line.**

1. (**6**) What is the Supreme Law of the Land? _____ the Constitution _____________

2. (   ) What is the highest court of the land? _________________________________

3. (   ) What branch of government makes the laws of the nation? _______________

4. (   ) How many Senators and Representatives does each state have in Congress? _______

5. (   ) Do U.S. residents have the same rights in all states? _________________

6. (   ) Who is the chief executive of the nation and Commander in Chief of the armed forces?

7. (   ) What are two ways to propose a Constitutional Amendment? _____________

8. (   ) What are some of the duties and powers of the President? _____________
____

9. (   ) What is one important responsibility of the Supreme Court? _____________

10. (   ) What form of government do the states have? _______________________

11. (   ) May a state constitution or judge contradict the U.S. Constitution? _______

12. (   ) How are new states admitted to the Union? _________________________

13. (   ) Who has to approve a proposed amendment? _________________________

14. (   ) What must public officials promise in an official oath? _______________
____

15. (   ) How many states had to ratify the Constitution before it became law? _______

 **The Amendments**

The U.S. Constitution is "a living document" because Americans can change it with amendments. The existing amendments protect individual rights or have solved other national problems.

Amendment	Ratified	What does the amendment say?
1-10	1791	The first ten amendments are the "Bill of Rights." (See Module 6B.)
11	1798	Citizens of a state or foreign country may not take another state to court.
12	1804	Electors vote for the President and Vice President on separate ballots.
13	1865	Slavery is illegal.
14	1868	All people born in the United States or naturalized are citizens.
15	1870	Black men have the right to vote.
16	1913	Congress has the right to tax income.
17	1913	The citizens elect U.S. Senators directly.
18	1919	It is illegal to make or sell liquor.
19	1920	Women citizens have the right to vote.
20	1933	A new President takes office on January 20.
21	1933	The Eighteenth Amendment was repealed.
22	1951	Presidents may serve no more than two terms.
23	1961	Citizens living in Washington D.C. may vote in Presidential elections.
24	1964	It is illegal to require voting taxes.
25	1967	The Vice President becomes President if the President can't carry out his duties.
26	1971	All citizens eighteen years and older may vote.

F **Make sentences about the information in E. You can use these sentence patterns.**

1. The _________________ Amendment was ratified in _________________.
       (number)   (year)

2. It says that ____.

Module 6B: Basic Rights and Freedoms

A Work in groups. Discuss these questions about individual rights in the United States and decide on the answers. Then check them on the next page.

1. If a reporter writes an article about a government official stealing money, can the newspaper publish it legally?
    a. Yes, because the Bill of Rights of the U.S. Constitution guarantees freedom of speech and the press.
    b. No, because the truth can damage the government.

2. Is Christianity the official religion of the United States?
    a. Yes, because most Americans are Christian.
    b. No, because separation of church and state is a principle of the U.S. government, and the Bill of Rights guarantees freedom of religion.

3. If you and your neighbors want to have a political meeting, how can you get permission from the government?
    a. You can call the mayor's office or write the state legislature.
    b. You don't need permission because you have the right to meet for any peaceful purpose.

4. If you oppose a federal law, what can you do about it?
    a. Nothing. You can protest local laws but not federal ones.
    b. You can write a letter to a government representative.

5. Who can own guns in the United States?
    a. All U.S. citizens if they follow the state laws about weapons.
    b. No one, because private gun ownership is illegal.

6. Who must allow soldiers to live in their homes?
    a. No one, except perhaps in time of war.
    b. All citizens, because this is a basic right of government.

7. How can you find out all your rights and freedoms?
    a. You can read the Constitution and law books, ask government officials, and talk to lawyers.
    b. All of these are in the Constitution and its Amendments.

8. How are the rights of born citizens different from the rights of naturalized citizens?
    a. They are the same, except that naturalized citizens can't become President of the U.S.
    b. Only born citizens can work in government jobs, join political parties, or run for office.

9. Is it legal for adults to use alcohol in the U.S.?
    a. No, because Amendment 18 made it illegal to make or sell liquor.
    b. Yes, because Amendment 21 repealed Amendment 18.

10. Who can register to vote in the United States?
    a. All born and naturalized citizens over the age of 18.
    b. Only white men in the fifty states (not in Washington, D.C.)

In your groups, discuss these sentences and decide on the correct words. Then check your answers at the bottom of this page.

Suppose you are charged with (accused of) a serious crime.

1. The police can enter your home to search it [with / without] a search warrant.

2. There [must / doesn't have to] be an official charge against you by a grand jury before your case goes to trial.

3. The government [can / can't] bring you to trial more than once for the same crime.

4. You [may / won't] have to testify against yourself.

5. The government [can / can't] take your property as punishment without payment or a legal process.

6. Your trial [may / can't] be secret and closed.

7. The Constitution [guarantees / doesn't guarantee] your right to a trial by jury.

8. The twelve jurors [must / don't have to] come to a unanimous verdict.

9. The government [must / doesn't have to] explain the charges against you.

10. You [have / don't have] the right to a lawyer.

11. You [may / can't] hear and question the witnesses against you.

12. You [can / can't] call witnesses to testify for you.

13. The judge can't demand [any / unfair] bail or charge fines [lower / much higher] than the cost of the crime or damage.

14. If you are guilty, there are [no / some] limits on the possible kinds of punishment.

Answers to Exercises A and B:

A   1. a 2. b 3. b 4. b 5. a 6. a 7. a 8. a 9. b 10. a

B   1. with 2. must 3. can't 4. won't 5. can't 6. can't 7. guarantees 8. must 9. must
10. have 11. can 12. can 13. unfair, much higher 14. some

To figure out the meanings of the words on the left, look back at the sentences in B. (The number in parentheses refers to the item.) Then match the words with their meanings on the right. Write the letters on the lines.

1. __**b**__ a search warrant (1)

   a. people who examine evidence to decide if a trial is necessary

2. ___ charge (noun) (2)

   b. legal permission to search

3. ___ grand jury (2)

   c. members of a jury who hear evidence and come to a verdict

4. ___ a trial (2)

   d. an accusation of a crime

5. ___ testify (4)

   e. people who give evidence

6. ___ guarantee (7)

   f. promise or give assurance

7. ___ jurors (8)

   g. money paid to guarantee that someone freed from jail will return to the trial

8. ___ a unanimous verdict (8)

   h. the hearing of a case in court

9. ___ witnesses (11)

   i. give evidence

10. ___ bail (13)

   j. decision agreed on by everyone

D   **Write the words from the list on the left in C.**

There are Constitutional Amendments to (1) __**guarantee**__ justice and fairness. Even if a (2) _______________ brings a (3) _____________ of a crime against you, you still have rights. For example, the police can't search your home without (4) _______________. They may free you from jail if someone pays your (5) ___________. You have a right to (6) ______________ before twelve (7) __________, and they must come to (8) ___________________. You don't have to (9) __________ against yourself, and you can hear the evidence of (10) _____________.

 **Here is a summary of the Constitutional Amendments about individual rights and liberties. To match each with the information in A and B, write the letter of the exercise and the number of the item on the line. (One amendment may refer to more than one item.) Then explain the amendments.**

1. A1,A2,A3,A4 Amendment 1 guarantees the right of freedom of speech, press, religion, peaceable assembly, and requesting change from the government.

2. _________ Amendment 2 guarantees the right to own weapons.

3. _________ Amendment 3 says that the government may not force people to take soldiers into their homes in peacetime.

4. _________ Amendment 4 says that the government may not search or take individual property without a warrant.

5. _________ Amendment 5 says that to bring a person to trial, a grand jury must charge him or her with a crime. Also, the government may not bring a person to trial more than once for the same crime and may not take away property without a legal process. No one must testify against himself or herself in court.

6. _________ Amendments 6 and 7 give individuals the right to an open trial by jury and a lawyer. They have the right to hear the charges, to question witnesses, and to get witnesses to testify for them.

7. _________ Amendment 8 protects people against unreasonable bail or fines and cruel or unusual punishment.

8. _________ Amendment 9 says that individuals have rights in addition to those in the Constitution.

9. _________ Amendment 14 guarantees all the rights of citizens to people born or naturalized in the U.S.

10. _________ Amendment 15 guarantees the right to vote to ex-slaves and black people.

11. _________ Amendment 18 made it illegal to make or sell alcohol.

12. _________ Amendment 19 guaranteed the right to vote to women.

13. _________ Amendment 21 repealed Amendment 18.

14. _________ Amendment 23 gives the right to vote to residents of Washington, D.C.

15. _________ Amendment 26 gives the right to vote to all citizens over the age of eighteen.

Module 7A: Overview of U.S. Government

A The American System of Government

The United States is a democratic republic (a representative democracy). The national government is a government of all the people and their representatives (elected officials). It is called the federal government because the nation is a federation, or association, of states.

The U.S. Constitution gave the federal government only limited powers, the powers stated in the Constitution. All other powers belong to the individual states.

The Founding Fathers established three branches of government: the legislative, the executive, and the judicial. Each branch has different functions and powers under the principle of separation of powers. There is also a system of checks and balances so that each branch has some control over the other two branches. This way, no one group can have too much power.

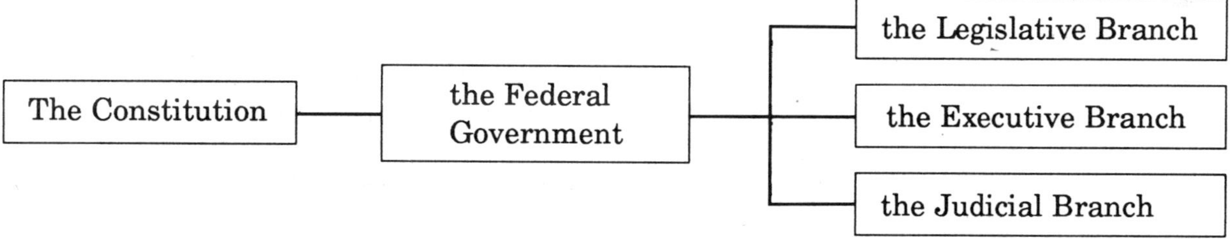

B Match the words with their meanings. Write the letters on the lines.

1. ___ a democratic republic

2. ___ representatives and senators

3. ___ the Federal Government

4. ___ a federation

5. ___ limited powers

6. ___ the branches of government

7. ___ the separation of powers

8. ___ checks and balances

a. an association

b. having different functions

c. the legislative, the executive, and the judicial

d. only those powers stated in the Constitution

e. a government of the people (a representative democracy)

f. elected officials

g. the national government

h. a system of control of each branch over the other two

 **The Three Branches of Government**

The legislative branch is called Congress. It consists of the Senate and the House of Representatives. It is the responsibility of Congress to propose and pass laws. In the system of checks and balances, Congress can refuse to approve Presidential appointments and can override a Presidential veto.

The executive branch consists of the President, the Vice President, the Cabinet and the thirteen Departments, and the independent agencies. It's the responsibility of the executive to enforce laws. The President has the power to veto (reject) any bill (law) of Congress. He appoints all Supreme Court Justices.

The judicial branch consists of the Supreme (highest) Court, eleven Circuit Courts of Appeals, and ninety-four District Courts. This branch explains and interprets laws and makes decisions in lawsuits. It has power over the other two branches because it can declare their laws and actions unconstitutional (against the principles of the Constitution).

 **Answer these questions about the three branches of government.**

	the Legislative	the Executive	the Judicial
1. What does it consist of?	the Senate the House of Representatives		
2. What are its responsibilities?			
3. What powers does it have under the system of checks and balances?			

E Political Parties

The U.S. Constitution does not talk about political parties, but they began during George Washington's term of office. On one side were the Federalists. They wanted a strong federal government. On the other side, the Democratic-Republicans wanted to limit the power of the national government. Their leader was Thomas Jefferson, and their group later became the Democratic Party.

Some of the early political parties, such as the Federalists and the Whigs, no longer exist. Since 1854, the two major parties have been the Democrats and the Republicans. Smaller parties have lasted for only a short time. "Third parties" have won in local elections, but their candidates have never won a Presidential election.

Many people say that there is not much difference between the Republican and Democratic Parties. "Liberal" politicians usually favor reform (change) and progress. "Conservative" politicians usually oppose change. But both liberal and conservative members belong to the two major political parties, and their ideas often change with the times and the issues.

F   Write **T** for true and **F** for false. Correct the false sentences.

1. ___ Article 2 of the U.S. Constitution establishes political parties.

2. ___ During the time of George Washington, the Federalists supported a strong federal government, but the Democratic-Republicans wanted to limit government power.

3. ___ Thomas Jefferson was the leader of the Whigs, a third party in opposition to change.

4. ___ Since 1854, the two major political parties have been the Whigs and the Libertarians.

5. ___ Voters have elected some third-party candidates to local office but never to the Presidency.

6. ___ All Democrats are conservative and all Republicans are liberals.

7. ___ Liberal politicians usually support reform, and conservative candidates oppose it.

8. ___ Political parties, candidates, and their ideas have changed with the times and the issues.

 **Work in pairs. Each of you studies the information about a different one of the two major political parties. Summarize your information for your partner.**

1.  The Democratic Party is the oldest party in the United States. In 1828 Andrew Johnson became the first Democratic President. Since that time, the issues of the nation and the ideas of the party have changed. Both the major parties have liberal and conservative members, but in general people consider the Democrats today more liberal than the Republicans. Democrats often want the government to establish social programs for people in need, such as the poor, the unemployed, and the elderly. They usually say they believe in equal rights for women and minorities and they oppose nuclear weapons and too much military spending. The symbol of the Democratic Party (from political cartoons) is the donkey.

2.  The Republican Party, sometimes called the G.O.P. (the Grand Old Party) began in 1854 over the issue of slavery. Republicans opposed slavery. The first Republican candidate to become President was Abraham Lincoln. After the Civil War, Republicans got interested in farm, land, and business issues. In general, Republicans vote more conservatively than Democrats. They want government to support big business but not to control the lives of citizens. They often oppose government spending for social programs but support military spending. The party symbol is the elephant.

 **Which party is each sentence about? Write R for the Republican and D for the Democratic.**

1. ___ It is the oldest political party in the United States.

2. ___ It is sometimes called the G.O.P.

3. ___ Its first President was Abraham Lincoln.

4. ___ Its first President was Andrew Johnson.

5. ___ It is generally more liberal than the other party.

6. ___ Its members usually prefer to spend tax money for military purposes rather than for social programs.

7. ___ Its members do not want the government to control the lives of individuals.

8. ___ The party symbol is the donkey.

I **Tell about other political parties in the United States or your native country.**

 # Module 7B: The Legislative Branch

A **Work in pairs or groups. Discuss these questions about the legislative branch of the federal government and decide on the answers. Then check your answers on page 84.**

1. What is the legislative branch of U.S. government called?
   a. Congress
   b. Parliament

2. What is a "bicameral" legislature?
   a. one with cameras
   b. one with two houses (divisions)

3. What are the two houses of Congress?
   a. the Council and the Supreme Soviet
   b. the Senate and the House of Representatives

4. Who is President of the Senate? (What is his office?)
   a. Mayor of Washington, D.C.
   b. Vice President of the U.S.

5. Who presides if the President of the Senate is absent?
   a. the President pro tempore
   b. the Vice President of the U.S.

6. Who presides over the House of Representatives (the House)?
   a. the President of the U.S.
   b. the Speaker of the House

7. What party does the Speaker of the House usually belong to?
   a. no political party
   b. the majority political party

B **Facts About Congress**

	the Senate	the House
Number of Members	100	435
Number of Members Per State	2	determined by state population
Length of Term	6 years[1]	2 years[1]
Number of Terms	no limit	no limit
Age Requirement	at least 30	at least 25
Citizenship Requirement	at least 9 years as a U.S. citizen	at least 7 years as a U.S. citizen
Dates of Regular Session	January 3 to adjournment	January 3 to adjournment

[1] One-third of all Senators and all Representatives run for office every two years.

C Make sentences about the information in B with these sentence patterns.

1. The | Senate / House of Representatives | has __________ members.
   (number)

2. The number of | Senators / Representatives | for each state is __________.

3. Each | Senator / Representative | serves in Congress for _________ years.
   (number)

4. There is ______ on the number of terms for each | Senator. / Representative.

5. To run for Congress, a | Senator / Representative | must be at least ________ years old
   (number)

   and a U.S. citizen for at least________ years.
   (number)

6. A regular session of the | Senate / House | is from __________ to _________.
   (date)

D Write the words from the chart on the next page.

1. To begin the law-making process, either a __**Senator**__ or a ________________ can write
   a __________.

2. The bill then goes to a _____________ of the same house.

3. The committee can call ________________________, ___________ (postpone) the bill, send it
   back to the full house without a __________________, or ___________ (change) the bill.

4. If the Senate or House _____________ the bill, it does not become law.

5. If the Senate or House _____________ the bill, it goes to the other house of Congress and its
   committee.

6. If the second house passes the bill, it goes to _____________.

7. If the President signs the bill, it ________________________.

8. If the President __________ (rejects) the bill, Congress can _____________ the veto, and it
   becomes law anyway.

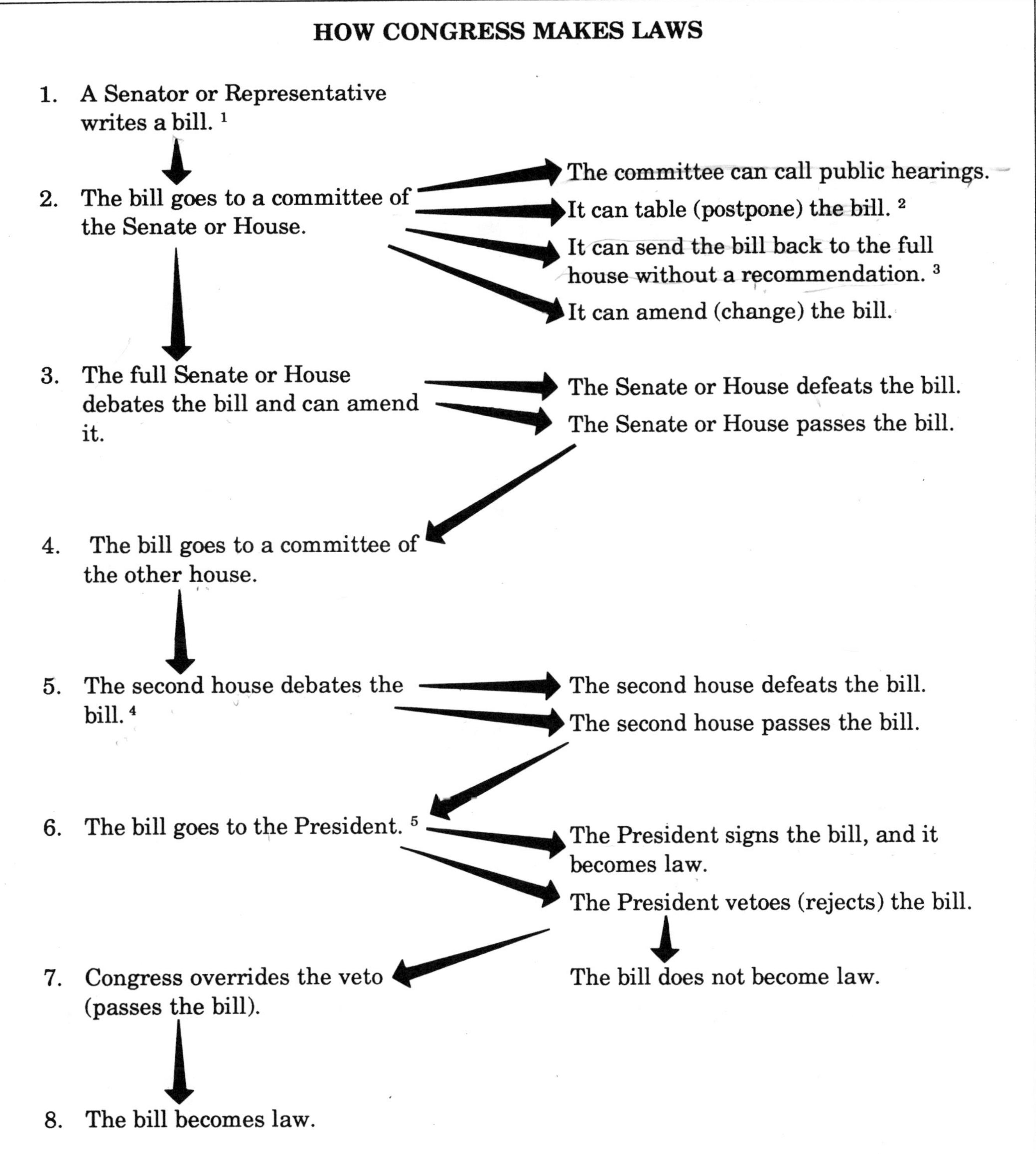

[1] A bill concerning taxes or the budget must begin in the House of Representatives.

[2] If a committee tables a bill, Senators or Representatives can force it out of committee with a majority vote.

[3] This step often "kills" the bill.

[4] If the second house of Congress amends the bill, the first house must agree to the changes.

[5] If the President does nothing and Congress adjourns within ten days, the bill does not become law.

 **What do you know about the members of Congress from your state? In pairs or small groups, find out the answers to these questions and write them in the chart. Discuss them with the class.**

	Senator 1	Senator 2	the Representative for your district
1. Who represents your state in Congress? [1]			
2. What political party does he or she belong to?			
3. How long has he or she served in Congress?			
4. Is he or she a "liberal" or a "conservative?"			
5. How do you know? (Give examples from his or her voting record.) [2]			

F   In small groups, discuss your answers to these questions.

1. How powerful is your state in Congress? (How many Representatives does it have?)

2. What are the important federal issues in your state?

3. What are the important federal issues in your Congressional district?

[1] Both Senators represent the whole state. A Representative represents one Congressional district.

[2] You can get information about the voting records of members of Congress from their local offices and from past issues of your local newspaper.

Answers to Exercise A: 1. a 2. b 3. b 4. b 5. a 6. b 7. b

Module 7C: The Executive Branch

A **Work in pairs. Look only at this page and ask your partner these questions about the President of the United States. Your partner will tell you the answers from the next page. Take notes on the information.**

1. What are the qualifications (requirements) for President?

2. What are the qualifications for Vice President?

3. For how many years may a President serve?

4. If the President dies, who becomes President?

5. Where does the President live and work?

6. How should people address the President?

B **Work in pairs. Look only at this page and tell your partner the steps in electing a President.**

1. Political parties choose their candidates in state caucuses (conventions) or state primaries (elections).

2. Political parties hold national conventions to choose their candidates for President and Vice President. Convention delegates vote for the choices of the voters in their states.

3. All candidates campaign until election day, the first Tuesday after the first Monday in November. Then the voters make their choices.

4. Electors (members of the Electoral College) cast their votes for President and Vice President. The candidates with the majority (more than half) of the electoral votes win.

5. If no candidate wins the majority of the electoral votes, the House of Representatives chooses the new President.

6. The new President takes office during the inauguration (formal ceremony) on January 20 after the election.

Work in pairs. Look only at this page. To answer your partner's questions about the President, find the information and tell it to your partner. He or she will take notes.

- The President travels a lot, but he or she lives and works at the White House in Washington, D.C.

- The President's term of office is four years, and no President may serve for more than two terms in a row.

- To qualify to serve, the President must be a born U.S. citizen and at least thirty-five years old. He or she must have lived in the United States for at least fourteen years.

- Visitors address him as Mr. President.

- The qualifications for Vice President are the same as the qualifications for President.

- If the President dies, these officials take over the position in this order: the Vice President, the Speaker of the House of Representatives, the President pro tempore of the Senate, the Secretary of State, the other twelve members of the Cabinet.

B   **Work in pairs. Your partner will tell you the steps in electing a President. Number them 1-6 on the lines in correct order.**

_____   Electors (members of the Electoral College) cast their votes for President and Vice President. The candidates with the majority of the electoral votes win.

_____   Political parties hold national conventions to choose their candidates for President and Vice President. Convention delegates vote for the choices of the voters in their states.

_____   The new President takes office during the inauguration (formal ceremony) on January 20 after the election.

_____   If no candidate wins the majority of the electoral votes, the House of Representatives chooses the new President.

_____   All candidates campaign until election day, the first Tuesday after the first Monday in November. Then the voters make their choices.

_____   Political parties choose their candidates in state caucuses (conventions) or state primaries (elections).

In your own words, tell the steps in electing a President.

D The Electoral College

U.S. citizens do not vote on federal laws because the U.S. system of government is a representative democracy, but they do choose the President and Vice President of the United States. However, the system of electing these officials is an indirect one.

When voters choose candidates on election day, they are actually voting for presidential "electors." The numbers of electors in each state is equal to the number of senators and representatives from that state in Congress. Because states with large populations have more representatives than states with fewer people, they have more power in an election. The Electoral College is based on a "winner-take-all" system. The winner of the majority of votes in each state gets all of that state's electoral votes. For example, the candidate with over fifty percent of the popular (total) vote in California gets all of that state's forty-seven votes, even if he or she won with only a small majority.

Because of the Electoral College system, occasionally the candidate with the majority of the popular vote loses the presidential election. This event is unusual, however.

In December the electors meet in their state capitals to cast their votes and send them to the U.S. Senate. On January 6 the members of Congress meet to count the votes.

E Write **T** for true and **F** for false. Correct the false sentences.

1. ___ U.S. citizens vote on federal laws, but they can't vote for Presidential or Vice Presidential candidates.

2. ___ Voters choose the President and the Vice President of the United States directly through the popular vote.

3. ___ Large states have more electoral votes than small states because their number of electors depends on the number of senators and representatives from the state in Congress.

4. ___ Candidates receive the same percentage of electoral votes from each state as their percentage of popular vote.

5. ___ Even if a candidate receives forty-nine percent of the votes in a state, he or she "loses" the state (gets no electoral votes) in a "winner-take-all" system.

6. ___ The candidate with the majority of the popular vote can still lose the national election.

7. ___ The electors of the Electoral College meet to cast their votes, and the members of Congress meet to count them.

 **The Cabinet, the Departments, and the Agencies**

It is the responsibility of the executive branch of the federal government to enforce the U.S. Constitution and federal laws. The President is Chief Executive and head of the government. The Vice President, the thirteen Cabinet members (usually called Secretaries) and their Departments, and the federal agencies are also part of the executive branch.

The President chooses the members of his Cabinet (the heads of the departments), and the Senate approves his choices. The fourteen departments are the Departments of:

State	the Interior	Health and	Transportation
the Treasury	Agriculture	Human Services	Education
Defense	Commerce	Housing and Urban	Energy
Justice	Labor	Development	Veterans' Affairs

Many federal agencies provide special services and may be temporary. Some well-known agencies are the the Civil Rights Commission, the Environmental Protection Agency, the Federal Trade Commission (FTC), the National Aeronautics and Space Administration, the United States Postal Service, and the Veterans Administration (VA).

G   **Write T for true and F for false. Correct the false sentences.**

1. _____   The executive branch makes laws but does not enforce them.

2. _____   The Vice President, the Chief Executive of government, chooses the members of the Cabinet with the approval of the voters.

3. _____   There are fourteen government departments, and their heads are usually called Secretaries.

4. _____   The State Department, the Department of the Treasury, and the Department of Commerce are some federal agencies.

H   **Do you remember or can you guess the functions of the officials and the departments and agencies of the executive branch? Complete this sentence in various ways.**

EXAMPLE: It is the responsibility of the Department of State to advise the President in foreign policy.

It is the responsibility of _________________ to _____________________.

 Module 7D: The Judicial Branch

A **Work in groups. Discuss these questions about the judicial branch of the federal government and decide on the answers. Then check your answers on the next page.**

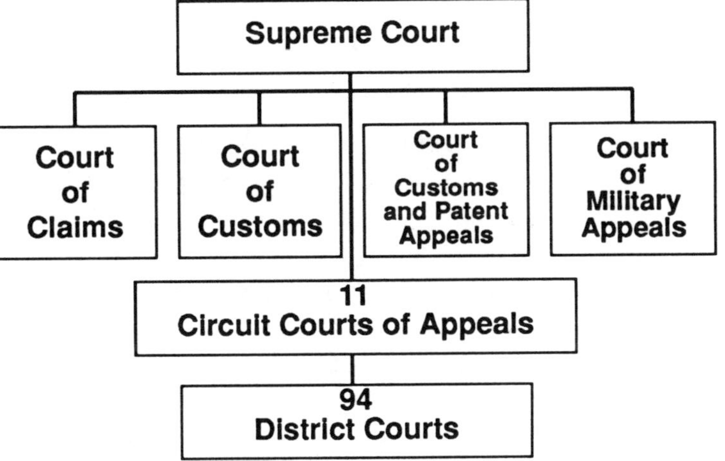

1. What is the highest court of the land?
    a. the Supreme Court
    b. the Presidential Tribunal

2. The Supreme Court is the "Last Court of Appeal." What does this mean?
    a. No other court has higher decision-making power.
    b. Citizens can appeal its decision (take the same case) to lower courts.

3. What does the Supreme Court do?
    a. It approves or overturns decisions of lower courts and explains and interprets laws.
    b. It hears cases from individual citizens without lawyers.

4. In the system of checks and balances, how does the judicial branch have power over the other two branches of government?
    a. The Supreme Court appoints all judges.
    b. The Supreme Court can decide on the constitutionality of laws and Presidential actions.

5. Where is the Supreme Court?
    a. in every state capitol
    b. in Washington, D.C. (the nation's capital)

6. Who chooses the justices of the Supreme Court?
    a. The voters elect them.
    b. The President appoints them, but the Senate must approve them.[1]

7. Who chooses the Chief Justice (head judge) of the Supreme Court?
    a. the President and the Cabinet
    b. The nine justices of the Supreme Court elect him or her.

[1]As an example, in 1987 the Senate rejected President Reagan's candidate, Robert H. Bork, because the Democrats (the majority party) thought he was too conservative.

8. Has there ever been a woman Supreme Court justice?
   a. Yes. Sandra Day O'Connor became the first woman justice in 1981.
   b. No, because the Constitution states that all Supreme Court justices must be men.

9. How long do Supreme Court justices serve?
   a. for the same length of time as senators from their states
   b. for life

10. Must the Supreme Court hear all appeals from lower courts?
    a. Yes, because hearing appeals is its only responsibility.
    b. No. It takes only the more important cases (especially cases concerning individual rights and the constitutionality of laws or actions).

11. Can the President or Congress abolish the Supreme Court?
    a. Yes, with a two-thirds majority of both houses.
    b. No. Only a Constitutional Amendment could abolish it.

12. What other kinds of courts and how many of them are there in the federal system?
    a. eleven Circuit Courts of Appeal and ninety-four District Courts
    b. two Executive Courts and three Legislative Courts

13. Are there any special federal courts?
    a. Yes. There are a Court of Claims, a Court of Customs, a Court of Customs and Patent Appeals, and a Court of Military Appeals.
    b. No. All courts must accept all kinds of cases.

14. What do the Circuit Courts of Appeals do?
    a. They hear appeals (requests to hear the case again) from lower courts.
    b. They overturn decisions of the Supreme Court.

15. What are the District Courts and what happens in them?
    a. They are state courts. All cases concerning state laws begin there.
    b. They are the lowest level of federal courts. Federal cases begin there.

16. How do federal courts differ from other courts?
    a. Federal courts take only cases concerning federal law. Other courts hear cases about state or local law.
    b. There is no difference. All courts take the same kinds of cases.

Answers to Exercise A: 1. a 2. a 3. a 4. b 5. b 6. b 7. b 8. a 9. b 10. b 11. b 12. a 13. a 14. a 15. b 16. a

 **Supreme Court Decisions**

Supreme Court decisions are very important to the nation because they set precedents. They serve as a guide in law making and the future decisions of all courts. Here are some examples.

Year	Case	Decision
1803	Marbury v. Madison	The Supreme Court has the right to interpret laws and judge their constitutionality.
1824	Gibbons v. Ogden	Only Congress can regulate interstate commerce (trade between states).
1832	Worchester v. Georgia	No state may control Indian Lands.
1941	"Poor Migrants"	It is unconstitutional for states to control or stop migration (movement) of people from one state to another.
1954	Brown v. the Board of Education of Topeka, Kansas	Segregated schools are unconstitutional because they are unequal. Integration (the bringing together of different races) is a part of education.
1963	Gideon v. Wainwright	Even in small cases, the government must provide a lawyer to a defendent (person on trial) if he or she can't afford one.
1964 / 1966	Escobedo v. Illinois / Miranda v. Arizona	The police must tell an arrested person about his or her right to remain silent and to have an attorney (lawyer) present when he or she answers questions.
1971	"Women's Rights"	Unequal treatment based on sex violates (goes against) the Fourteenth Amendment.
1973	Roe v. Wade	States cannot make abortion illegal, except in the later stages of pregnancy.
1981	Rotsker v. Goldberg	Congress may draft (take for military service) only men (not women) into the armed forces.
1982	Plyer v. Doe	Illegal (undocumented) aliens are persons under the Constitution and have the same protections under the law as citizens and residents.
1987	INS v. Cardoza-Fonseca	The U.S. government can give asylum (protection) to refugees if they have reason to fear death or mistreatment in their native countries. Refugees no longer have to prove that their lives are in danger.

 **In groups, read each situation and answer this question: Why would the Supreme Court disapprove of the situation? On the line, write the name and year of the Supreme Court case that is the precedent.**

1. _Plyer v. Doe (1982)_________________:
Texas keeps the children of illegal aliens out of its public schools.

2. ________________________________:
California taxes all goods from Nevada.

3. ________________________________:
Oregon refuses to let a family move there from Washington because they have no home and little money.

4. ________________________________:
Arizona sends a woman to jail because she went to the doctor to abort a two-month old fetus.

5. ________________________________:
Without permission, Nebraska takes land from an Indian reservation to build a state prison.

6. ________________________________:
A young man refuses to enter the U.S. Army because his sister does not have to serve in the armed forces.

7. ________________________________:
The police send a man to prison for drunk driving but do not give him an attorney because he can't afford one.

8. ________________________________:
A public university refuses to admit a student because she is not white.

9. ________________________________:
You are the best-qualified candidate for police chief but the city won't give you the job you because you are a woman.

10. ________________________________:
The INS sends a political refugee back to his country because he cannot prove that his government would take his life.

11. ________________________________:
The police arrest a man and tell him to confess his crime on videotape in a room with no one else present.

12. ________________________________:
Congress makes the Speaker of the House the head of the armed forces even though the Constitution gives that position to the President.

 **Do you know about other Supreme Court decisions? Tell the class.**

State Government

Module 8A: Branches of Government and Officials

A Work in pairs. Tell your partner each fact about the federal government and listen to the corresponding fact about state government. Write **S** on the line if the facts are the same for both governments. Write **D** if they are different.

1. **S** The federal government is in the form of a democratic republic, which means that the people elect representatives.
2. ___ It is a representative democracy because the people have the power through their elected representatives.
3. ___ The government follows the principles of a constitution with its bill of rights.
4. ___ The government has three branches with different responsibilities and powers.
5. ___ The legislative branch has two houses that make laws.
6. ___ The upper house is the Senate, and the lower house is the House of Representatives.
7. ___ The leaders of the executive branch are the U.S. President and Vice President.
8. ___ The President appoints the members of the Cabinet. These advisors ("Secretaries") are the heads of federal departments.
9. ___ The judicial branch of the federal government judges cases of federal law.
10. ___ The highest court is the U.S. Supreme Court. There are also circuit courts of appeals and district courts.

B From the information in A on this page, write the missing words in the boxes.

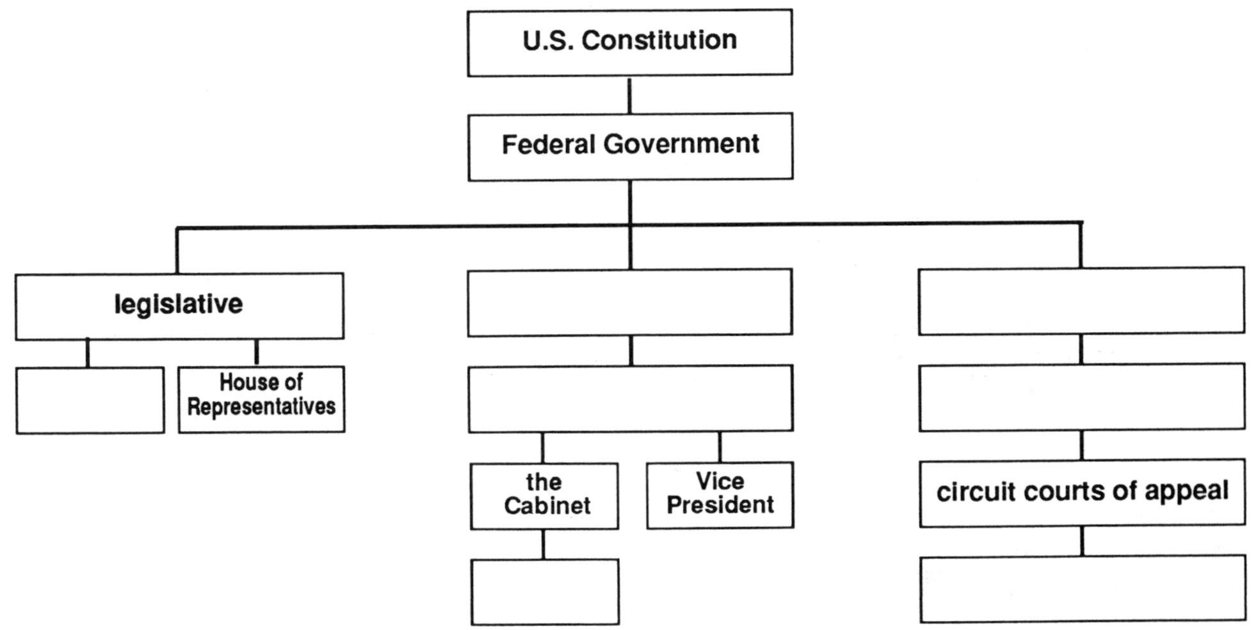

 **A** **Work in pairs. Tell your partner each fact about state government and listen to the corresponding fact about the federal government. Write S on the line if the facts are the same for both governments. Write D if they are different.**

1. __S__ State government is in the form of a democratic republic, which means that the people elect representatives.

2. ___ In addition to power through their elected state representatives, the people have direct power through the initiative, referendum, and recall processes.

3. ___ The government follows the principles of a constitution with its bill of rights.

4. ___ The government has three branches with different responsibilities and powers.

5. ___ The legislative branch has two houses that make laws.*

6. ___ The upper house is a senate, and the lower house is a state assembly or a house of representatives.

7. ___ The leaders of the executive branch are the governor and the lieutenant governor.

8. ___ The executive branch includes advisors to the governor. Some advisors are elected and some are appointed.

9. ___ The judicial branch of state government judges cases of state law.

10. ___ The highest court is the state supreme court. There may also be appellate (appeals), county, superior, district, circuit, municipal, and special courts.

C **From the information in A on this page, write the missing words in the boxes.**

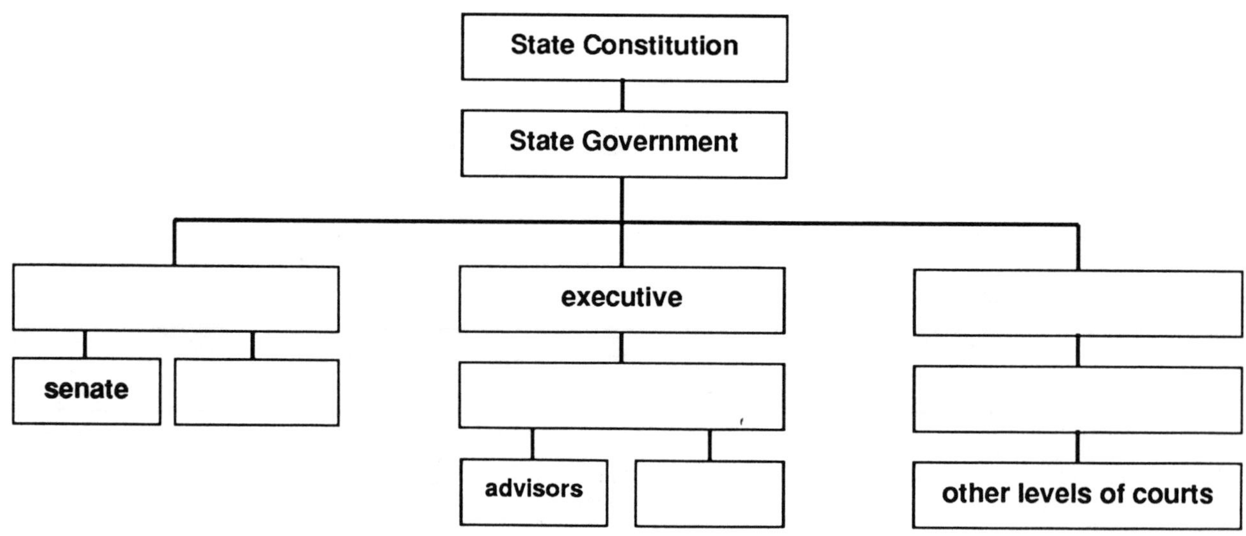

* Only Nebraska has a one-house state legislature.

 **Make sentences about the similarities and differences in federal and state government with these sentence patterns.**

EXAMPLES: 1. Both the federal and state governments are in the form of a republic. In both the federal and state governments, the people elect representatives.

        2. Both the federal and state governments are representative democracies because the people elect representatives. On the other hand, in state government, the people also have direct power in law making.

1. (In) Both the federal and state governments ________________.

2. (In) The federal government _______________________.

    On the other hand, (in) state government _____________________.

E **Read the information. Then find out the answers to the questions about the legislative branch of government in your state.**

Like the Congress of the United States, most state legislatures are bicameral because they consist of two houses, an upper and a lower one. A government leader such as the lieutenant governor or the speaker of the assembly presides over each house.

In some states, citizens elect legislators by population, so there is one representative for a certain number of people. In other states, all voters choose all representatives, so they are elected "at large." In still other states, elections are by district, and there are a certain number of representatives for each geographical area.

1. If you live in a state other than Nebraska, what is the name of the lower house of your state legislature (the house of representatives or the assembly)?

2. What state official presides over each house?

3. How do citizens in your state elect representatives (by population, by district, or "at large")?

4. How long is a term of office in each house?

5. How many members are there in each house?

6. Who are the state legislators from your area? What political parties do they belong to?

Read the information. Then find out the answers to the questions about the executive branch of government in your state.

The chief executive of a state is the governor. A lieutenant governor replaces the governor if he or she can no longer serve. In some states, the governor appoints his or her advisors, and in other states, the people elect them. High state officials may have different titles, but their responsibilities are similar in all states. For example, the Secretary of State keeps records and announces new laws. The Attorney General represents the state in court. The Treasurer receives tax money and pays bills for the state, and the Auditor or Comptroller is concerned with state financial matters. The Superintendant of Public Instruction is the highest officer in educational matters.

1. Who are the governor and lieutenant governor of your state? What political party do they belong to?

2. How long is their term of office? How many terms may they serve?

3. Name five high offices in the executive branch of your state. Are they elected or appointed positions?

4. Who holds the five positions? What do these officers do?

Find out the answers to these questions about the supreme court in your state. Then look at the chart and circle the names of the other courts in the judicial branch.

1. In what city or cities does the state supreme court meet?

2. How many judges are there in the state supreme court? Does the governor appoint them, or do the people elect them?

3. For how many years do they serve?

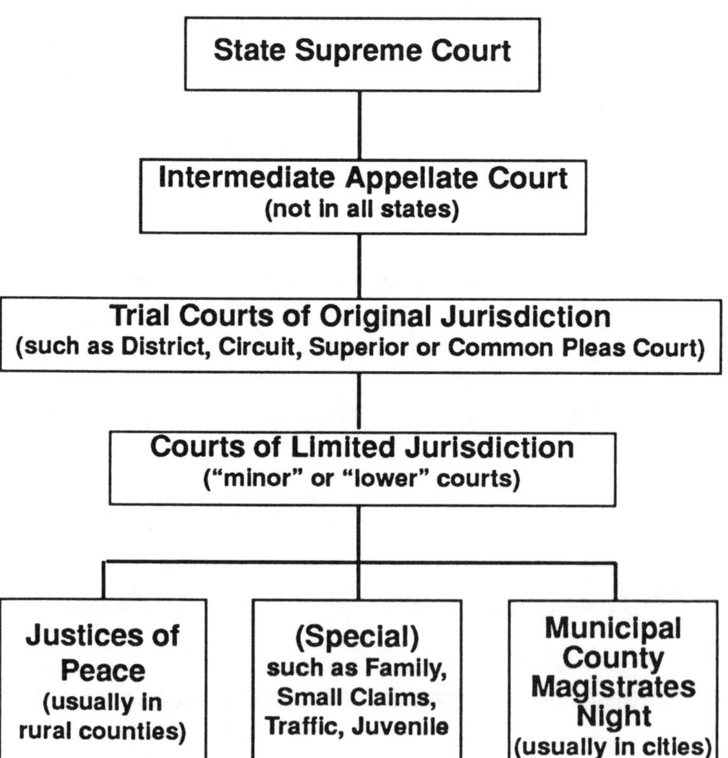

 Module 8B: Functions, Powers, and Services

A **Work in pairs. Look only at this page and answer your partner's questions about the responsibilities of the federal and state governments.**

Only the federal government:
- declares war
- supports the armed forces
- coins money
- establishes and maintains post offices
- gives authors and inventors the exclusive right to their work (copyrights or patents)
- makes treaties with the governments of other countries

Only a state government:
- maintains a police force
- supports a state militia, such as the National Guard
- regulates transportation and trade within the state
- establishes and maintains schools
- oversees local governments and grants city charters

Both the federal and state governments:
- fund public projects (buildings, dams, highways, etc.)
- support farming and business
- maintain court systems
- regulate banks

The federal government usually provides funding and the states distribute the money and provide programs for:
- public assistance for people in need
- health care
- protection of natural resources
- improvements in living and working conditions

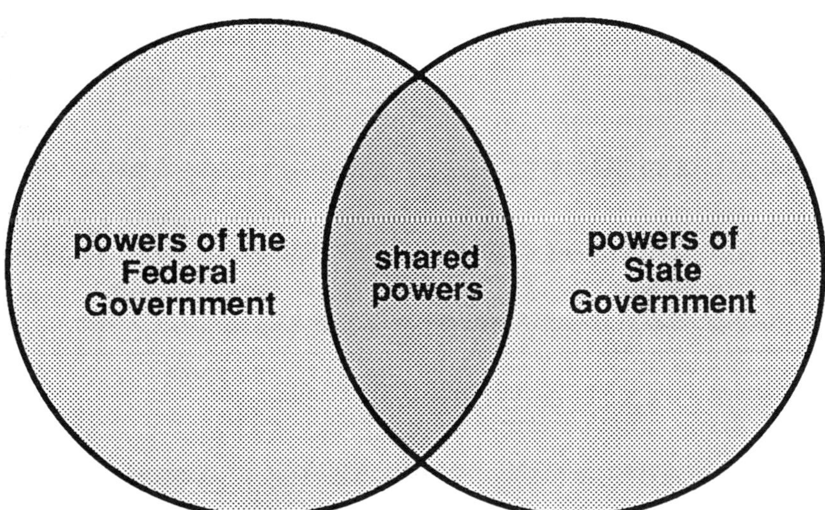

"The powers not delegated to the United States by the Constitution nor prohibited by it to the states are reserved to the states respectively, or to the people." The Tenth Amendment to the Constitution of the United States.

 **Work in pairs. Look only at this page and ask your partner questions with the pattern "Which government . . .s   . . .?" Write the answer or answers on the line.**

EXAMPLE: Student 1: Which government declares war and makes treaties?

Student 2: The federal government.

1.   . . . declares war and makes treaties? ________ **federal** ________

2.   . . . maintains a police force and state militia? ________________

3.   . . . regulates trade and transportation in the state? ________________

4.   . . . coins money and maintains post offices? ________________

5.   . . . establishes and maintains schools? ________________

6.   . . . regulates banks and supports business? ________________

7.   . . . oversees local government and grants city charters? ________________

8.   . . . funds public projects, like dams and highways? ________________

9.   . . . maintains court systems? ________________

10.   . . . issues copyrights and patents? ________________

11.   . . . provides public assistance and health care for people in need?

____

12.   . . . provides funding for the protection of natural resources?

____

13.   . . . distributes money through programs to improve living and working conditions?

____

B **Answer these questions in as many ways as you can.**

1. What can the federal government do that a state government can't? (Example: declare war).

2. What does a state do that the federal government doesn't do?

3. What do both the federal and state governments do?

4. What programs does the federal government provide funding for and state governments maintain?

C The Separation of Powers in State Government

State governments are similar in structure to each other and to the federal government. Under the principle of separation of powers, the government of each state has three branches—the legislative, the executive, and the judicial. In the system of checks and balances, each branch has some control over the other two branches.

The governor may veto bills from the legislature (the senate and the house or assembly). In some states, the governor uses a "line-item veto." This way, he or she does not have to reject an entire law in order to veto parts of it. The governor also appoints judges in the judicial branch. With enough votes in both houses, the legislature can override the governor's veto.

Like the federal courts, state courts also explain and interpret laws. They can declare state laws unconstitutional (contradictory to the state constitution).

State government includes a system of direct democracy. Through the initiative process, citizens may put proposed laws on the ballot for the people to vote on. They may decide on proposed constitutional amendments or important state issues in a referendum. Through a recall, they can sometimes remove an elected government official from office.

The federal government also has power over state governments. For example, a state constitution or court may not contradict the U.S. Constitution, and the U.S. Supreme Court may overrule the decision of a state supreme court. Also, the U.S. President may withhold money from a state if the state refuses to obey federal laws.

D Write T for true and F for false. Correct the false sentences.

1. ___ All state governments are similar to one another, but they are different in structure from the federal government.

2. ___ The principles of separation of powers and checks and balances apply to state as well as the federal government.

3. ___ In a "line-item veto," the governor can reject parts of initiatives, referendums, or recalls.

4. ___ Like in the federal government, state legislatures can override vetos, and state courts can declare laws unconstitutional.

5. ___ Citizens may propose laws, vote on constitutional amendments, and recall elected officials in the federal system of direct democracy but not in a state system.

6. ___ The U.S. Supreme Court and the U.S. President have some direct power over state governments.

How to Find Public Services

The executive branch of state government includes many offices (departments, commissions, and boards) to help the public. You can find their names, addresses, and telephone numbers in the front part of the white pages of your local telephone book. Here are examples from Los Angeles, California:

ALCOHOLIC BEVERAGE CONTROL DEPT
Licensing--Enforcment--Information
El Monte District 9350 Flair Dr
Rm 204...575-6901

ASSEMBLY
Assembly Speaker Willie L. Brown Jr.
107 S Broadway...620-4356

Alatorre Richard Assemblyman 55th
District 6801 N Figueroa 255-7111

CALIFORNIA COMMUNITY COLLEGES
107 S Broadway 620-2388

CONSUMER AFFAIRS DEPT OF
See White Pages under Consumer
Complaint and Protection Coordinators

CONTRACTORS STATE LICENSE BOARD
7100 Bowling Dr Sacramento
Suite 350...916 445-3458

EMPLOYMENT DEVELOPMENT DEPARTMENT
Job Service Downtown Los Angeles
Avalon 161 W Venice Bl 744- 2018

FRANCHISE TAX BOARD
Los Angeles Office 3200 Wilshire Bl

HOUSING AND EMPLOYMENT DISCRIMINATION
322 W 1st. 620-2610

MOTOR VEHICLES DEPT
8 AM To 5 PM Mon-Tue-Wed-Fri
8 AM To 6 30 PM Thur
Alhambra..575-8611
Bell...744-2000
Beverly Hills 271-4585

SOCIAL SERVICES DEPT OF
Public Inquiry & Response--Welfare
Complaints 107 S Broadway 620-4730
Welfare Client Assistance
No Charge to Calling Party 800 952-5253

Can you guess which state offices can help you solve these problems? In groups, decide on the California department, commission, or board to call in these situations.

1. You need help with state income tax forms.

2. You want information about a bill before it goes before the state assembly.

3. You want to complain about false advertising.

4. You want information about educational opportunities in public two-year colleges.

5. You and your neighbors want to complain about a local liquor store that sells beer to high school students.

6. You believe that it is difficult for your family to rent an apartment because you are from another country.

7. You need to find a job.

8. Your children want to apply for driver's licenses.

9. You need financial help because you have children and no job?

10. You need a license to become a building contractor.

In your local telephone book, find the names, addresses, and telephone numbers of the state offices to contact in the situations in F. Then discuss the purposes of other listed state departments, commissions, and boards.

Local Government

Module 9A: County and City Services

A Public Services

The names of the departments of county or city government may vary. However, in both large cities and small towns, these departments provide similar services to the public.

B Work in groups of five. Each of you studies the information in a different section. In turn, summarize the information in your own words for the group.

1.

In some cities, there are separate police and fire departments. But in other places, the Department of Public Safety includes a police bureau and a fire bureau.

In the police bureau, there may be a separate traffic division responsible for accident investigation, a detective division to examine the evidence in crimes, and an identification and laboratory section. Volunteer companies may fight fires in the county and in small towns, but the fire bureau of a city is a large professional unit.

2.

The Department of Public Safety may include a building inspector and a traffic engineer. The office of the building inspector issues construction permits to contractors. It sends out employees to inspect new and old buildings. These officials check for violations of the building code, the local rules for safety.

Employees of the city's traffic engineering bureau study traffic patterns and recommend places for one-way streets, traffic lights, stop signs, and so on.

3.

The Public Works Department is responsible for the maintenance of streets and sewers (pipes that carry wastes). Its employees clean the streets and collect garbage. Most cities hire private contractors for major construction projects and repairs.

The Department of Public Utilities usually provides water, gas, and electricity, and in some places, it runs transportation lines. It also operates water purification plants. Employees of the department read the utility meters on each building to determine monthly billing.

4.

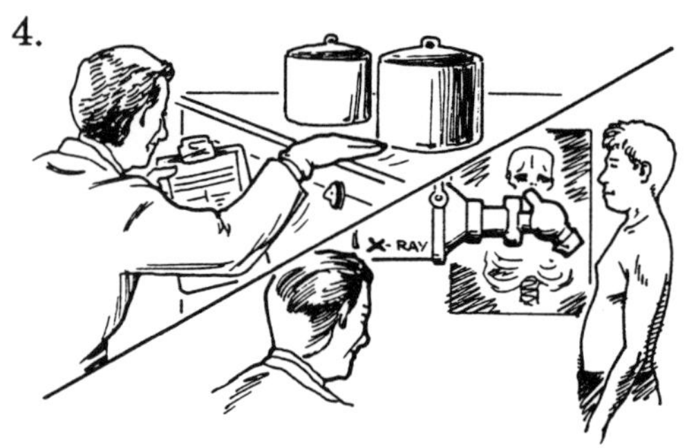

The Department of Public Health sends inspectors out to restaurants, food-processing plants, nursing homes, and similar places. If a place has violated local health or sanitation laws, the department issues warnings and instructions. It can impose penalties if violations are not corrected.

Other divisions of the health department run clinics that provide low-income people with free health services, such as chest X-rays, lab tests, and baby care. They may also offer health education.

5.

The Department of Social Services is concerned with the welfare of people who need help, such as young children, the disabled, the elderly, and the blind. Most of the money for these programs comes from state and federal tax funds.

The Department of Parks and Recreation maintains parks and other recreational facilities, such as community centers, swimming pools, tennis courts, and baseball fields. It may also provide recreational programs (instruction in sports, dances, classes, etc.).

C Correct these false sentences.

1. The services of local government departments differ from one city to another, but the names are always the same.

2. The Department of Public Safety may include social services and health inspection.

3. Volunteers run the fire departments or bureaus of large cities.

4. Most cities hire private contractors for minor maintenance of streets and sewers and for garbage collection.

5. The Department of Public Health has no power because it can't impose penalties for violations of sanitation laws.

6. The disabled, the elderly, and the blind provide funding for the programs of the Department of Social Services.

 **Work in pairs. Ask and answer questions about public services with these sentence patterns.**

EXAMPLE: Student 1: What does the traffic division of the police department do?

Student 2: It investigates accidents.

1. What | does / do | _______________________________ usually do?
(department, division, or people)

2. It / They | _______________________________ .
(description of service)

E What Can You Learn at City Hall?

Many cities offer guided tours of their seat of government, usually the city or town hall. You can also visit the local departments on your own to find out what they do. Here are some examples of questions you might ask.

The Finance Department

1. How much does it cost to run the city?

2. How does the city spend its money?

3. Where does the money come from?

4. How does the city borrow money?

The Commerce Department

1. How does the city attract new businesses?

2. What does the city offer visitors and tourists?

3. What public information services does the city offer?

4. How does the city "compete" with other cities?

The Law Department

1. What legal services does the city need?

2. In what situations must the city go to court?

3. What records does the city keep?

4. Can citizens sue the city? (If so, how?)

The City Planning Department

1. How does the city plan its growth?

2. What is zoning, and how does the city use it?

3. What does the city require from private developers?

4. What is the "Master Plan" of the city?

Transportation Department

1. What public transportation does the city provide?

2. Where does the city get transportation equipment?

3. How does the city plan its systems?

4. How does it get funding for those systems?

Personnel Department

1. How many employees work for the city?

2. How did they get their jobs?

3. What is the Civil Service system?

4. What is the salary range for city jobs?

 **As a class or in small groups, visit city hall or the seat of government in your town or county. Complete one or more of these activities and report on your experiences to the class.**

1. List the names of the city departments. Circle the departments with the same names as the departments mentioned in this module.

2. Choose one or more of the departments discussed in Exercise B. List at least four questions about it, similar to the questions in E. Visit the department and ask an employee the questions. If you think of more questions, ask them. Take notes on the answers. Summarize the information in a short report.

3. Choose one or more of the departments in E. Visit the department and ask an employee the questions. When he or she gives an interesting answer, ask more questions about that topic. Take notes and summarize the information in a short report.

4. Follow the instructions in (2) for another government department.

 **How to Find Public Services**

You can find the names, addresses, and telephone numbers of government offices in the front part of the white pages of your local telephone book. The offices are usually in a list under the title "City Government Offices" or "County Government Offices" and the name of the city or county. Here are examples from a city near Los Angeles, California.

WEST HOLLYWOOD CITY OF

GENERAL INFORMATION	**854-7400**
CITY CLERK	854-7408
Domestic Partnership Information-Election Info	854-7408
CITY COUNCIL	854-7460
CITY HALL 8611 Santa Monica Bl LA	854-7400
CITY MANAGER	854-7427
CITY CHANNEL 36	854-7388
COMMUNITY DEVELOPMENT	854-7475
Building & Safety	854-7320
Code Enforcement	854-7475
Economic Development	854-7475
Housing	854-7475
Planning & Zoning	854-7475
Transportation	854-7475
FINANCE DIVISION	854-7451
HUMAN SERVICES	854-7471
AIDS Information	854-7471
Fine Arts	854-7471
Recreation Services	854-7471
Senior Service-Referral	854-7471
Social Services	854-7471
LIBRARY	
Bouchardt Senior Citizens Library 1200 N Vista LA	851-8447
PARKS	
Plummer Park 1200 N Vista LA	876-1725
West Hollywood Park	652-3063
PERSONNEL	854-7325
24 Hour Job Hot Line	854-7309
POLICE DEPARTMENT	
Los Angeles County Sheriff West Hollywood Division	
Emergency Calls	911
Business Calls	855-8850
PUBLIC INFORMATION	854-7423
PUBLIC WORKS	854-7327
Contract Administration	854-7327
Engineering	854-7327
Service Requests	854-7327
Traffic Division	854-7327
Bus Pass Information	854-7327
RENT STABILIZATION	854-7450
Administration	854-7450
Hearings	854-7450

 **Work in pairs. Ask and answer questions with these sentence patterns about the telephone listings in G.**

1. What are the divisions or offices of the _________________?
   (department)

2. What does the ____________________________ usually do?
   (department or division)

 **Work in pairs. Repeat Exercise H with the listings for city or county government offices from your local telephone book.**

Module 9B: County Government

A   The Structure of County Government

County government is different in structure from state and federal government. The elected governing body has many different names throughout the country, but "board of supervisors" and "board of county commissioners" are two common ones.

A county board receives its authority from the county charter (official document to establish an organization). It not only passes ordinances (county laws), but it enforces them, too, along with state laws. The board may share executive powers with other elected officials such as the sheriff. County revenue comes from the federal and state governments, county property taxes, and other sources such as sales and income taxes and licensing.

A small county board has between five and eleven elected members, usually part-time officials. They meet in the county seat, a city or town in the county.

B   Here is some information about state government. Finish each sentence with the corresponding information about county government.

1. The elected governing body of the state is the state legislature, but the elected governing body of the county __has many different names, such as "board of supervisors"__.

2. The state government receives its authority from the state constitution, but the county board
   _______________________________________.

3. The state legislature passes state laws, but the county board
   _______________________________________.

4. The governor is the chief executive of the state, but the county board
   _______________________________________.

5. State revenue comes from state taxes, but county revenue
   _______________________________________.

6. The state legislature has hundreds of members, but a county board
   _______________________________________.

7. State legislators usually meet in the state capital, but county board members
   _______________________________________.

C   Other County Officials

In some counties, the voters elect officials, and in other counties, the board appoints them. The high officials in many counties have the same level of power as the elected board members. Here are some common titles for officials and their responsibilities.

Official	Responsibilities
County Attorney / District Attorney	• is the lawyer for the county • brings criminal cases to court
Sheriff	• provides police protection • oversees the county jails
Assessor	• determines property values so the county can set tax rates
Treasurer	• receives tax money • pays bills for the county
County Engineer	• plans and manages construction projects
Superintendant of Schools	• oversees county schools not part of city school systems
County Clerk*	• is an official recorder of county business • is secretary to the county board • issues birth certificates and marriage licenses

D   Work in pairs. Ask and answer questions about the responsibilities of county officials with these sentence patterns.

EXAMPLE: Student 1: What does the district attorney usually do?

Student 2: He or she is a lawyer for the county.

1. What does the ___________________ usually do?
   (official)

2. He | ____.
   She | (description of service)

* In large cities, there may be more than one recording office. In Los Angeles, for example, residents go to the Registrar-Recorder for family documents and voter registration.

E An Example of County Organization

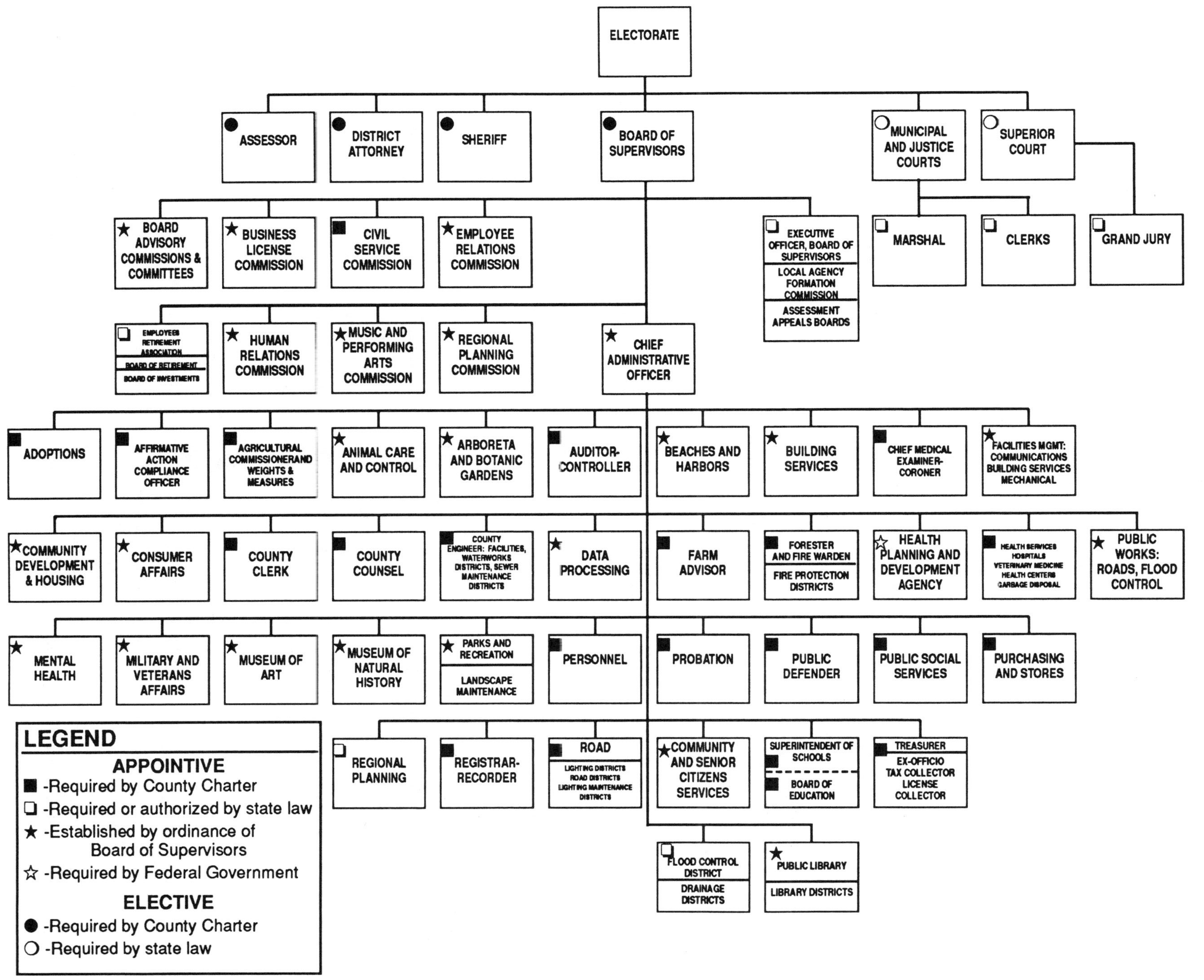

 **Work in pairs. Ask and answer these questions about the chart on the previous page.**

1. What officials are elected rather than appointed?

2. What officials have the same level of power as the members of the board of supervisors?

3. What are some examples of appointed positions required by state law? (See the Legend.)

4. What are some examples of high-level commissions?

5. What are some examples of departments or sections under the supervision of the chief administrative officer?

6. What are the special districts (organizations for large, expensive responsibilities)?
    ____

7. Which is higher on the organizational chart: (the) _______________________________ or (the)
                                                 (official or office)
    _______________________________?}
       (official or office)

8. What does (the) _______________________________ usually do?
                          (official or office)

9. (a question of your own)

 **Work in pairs. Ask and answer questions with this question pattern about the county budget charts.**

EXAMPLE: What percentage of county revenue comes from the state?

What percentage of county	revenue expenditures	comes from goes to	_______?

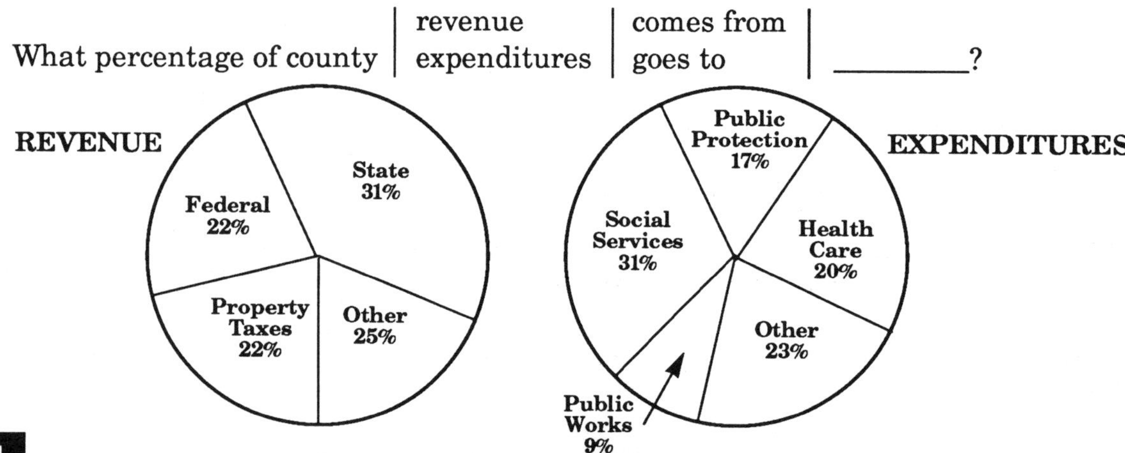

 **You can get information about your county from your local telephone book and a county "fact book" from the public library or the office of the district county supervisor. With this information, ask and answer questions about your county like those in F and G. Summarize the information for the class.**

 **Module 9C:** City Government

A The Structure of City Government

The government of a state grants city charters, and the charter establishes the form of local government. There are three main forms.

Law-Making Body	How Chosen?	Chief Executive	How Chosen?	Functions and Powers
city council	elected by the people	the mayor	elected by the people	may have actual power or be only a council member[1]
city council	elected	the city manager	hired by council	takes instructions from the council
commission	elected	one commissioner	chosen by commission	is the ceremonial head of government only[2]

B Make sentences about the information in A with these sentence patterns.

EXAMPLE: The city charter establishes the mayor-council form of government.

1. In one form of city government, the members of the _________________________ are
    (law-making body)

    _____________ by the voters.
    (how chosen?)

2. The chief executive, _____________________, is _____________________________.
    (title of official)   (how chosen?)

3. He or she _________________________________.
    (functions and powers)

C Make sentences about the form of government in your town or city with the patterns in B. Begin Sentence 1 with "In our form of city government, ..."

[1]In some cities, the mayor carries out the laws and is the most powerful local government leader. In other cities, the mayor is simply a council member who represents the city in ceremonies.

[2]All the commissioners are executive officers of the city, and one is the ceremonial head.

 **Getting Involved in Local Government**

In many countries, the national or central government runs the cities through its officials. But in the United States, local government means self-government. The state government creates cities and determines their responsibilities and powers, and no city council or commission may contradict its charter or state law. But the city may have a large amount of freedom, and every resident of the city has the opportunity to participate directly in local government.

 **Correct these false sentences.**

1. In the United States, the national government runs the cities through its officials.

2. The city council or commission can contradict its charter and state law in local matters because cities create themselves.

3. City residents cannot participate directly in local government because cities have no self-government.

F   **Walk around the classroom and ask your classmates these questions about their experiences in the United States and their native countries. When someone answers *yes*, write his or her name on the line. Then ask questions and write notes on the answers.**

Have you or someone you know ever. . .

1. . . . .run for local political office (Example: on a board of a special district)?

    ____

2. . . .supported a local candidate for office (Examples: by calling, visiting voters, or contributing money)? ____

3. . . .attended a city council, commission, or board meeting or heard one on the radio?

    ____

4. . . .supported or opposed a local issue? (How?) ____

5. . . .joined a public protest, such as a street demonstration? ______________________________

G **City residents can make important changes through neighborhood action. Divide the class into groups of "neighbors." Each group chooses a different one of the following local issues. Discuss the situation and suggest three or more solutions. Then tell the class your solutions and the reasons for them. The class will decide on the best one.**

1. There have been many accidents on the corner of your street because there is no stop sign.

2. Rainwater doesn't drain well on your street, and the street sweeper doesn't clean the street well because not all residents move their cars.

3. There have been several burglaries in your neighborhood recently, and you are especially afraid because your street is very dark at night.

4. You know that some residents in your building sell drugs, but you are afraid to call the police.

5. You live downtown and always see homeless people sleeping on the streets at night. The rents in the area are high.

6. Teenagers from the local high school cruise the main boulevard every Friday and Saturday night. They often get into fights, damage property, and write graffiti on walls.

7. (a situation of your own)

 **The Board of Education**

In some places, the city council appoints the board of education and controls school funding. But in most cities, the board is more independent of local government. It often has its own budget and may collect taxes. Sometimes its members are elected, and board meetings are open to the public.

Board members must make decisions on the many problems that face the school system. The public expresses its opinions in various ways. The views in this letter are typical:

```
Dear Members of the Board of Education:


We parents demand changes in the city school
system. There are too many students in each
classroom and too few teachers and other school
personnel to control them. Our schools are
becoming dangerous. Why don't school principals
expel students who disturb classes so that our
children can learn? Our sons and daughters
score low on national tests, but they seldom
have homework to do. If the situation does not
improve soon, this parents' organization will
sponsor a petition to recall the school board
members and elect new ones.


                Parents for Better Education
```

 **In small groups, pretend that you are members of the local school board. Discuss your answers to these questions. Together, write an answer to the letter in H.**

1. How much money is available for new teachers and other school personnel?

2. Are there classrooms available for more (smaller) classes? If not, how much money is available for new rooms or schools?

3. How might the community raise more money for education?

4. In the United States, every child has the right to a free public education. Can school principals expel students?

5. Are national test scores important? If so, how can teachers improve the scores of their students?

6. Should students have homework? If so, how much?

7. What are the responsibilities of parents in the education of their children?

The History of the United States

Module 10A: Overview of U.S. History

A Ten Periods of U.S. History

1.  Christopher Columbus discovered North America. European explorers and settlers came to the new land for gold, adventure, and freedom. The colonists lived under British laws.

| 1492 |
| 1500's |
| 1600's |

2.  Americans in the thirteen colonies wanted to be free of British rule. General George Washington led the colonists in the Revolutionary War. Thomas Jefferson wrote the Declaration of Independence, and the colonies approved it.

| 1775 |
| 1776 |

3.  The American colonists won the war, and the colonies became the United States of America. The Constitution became the highest law of the land, and George Washington became the first President.

| 1783 |
| 1787 |
| 1789 |

4. 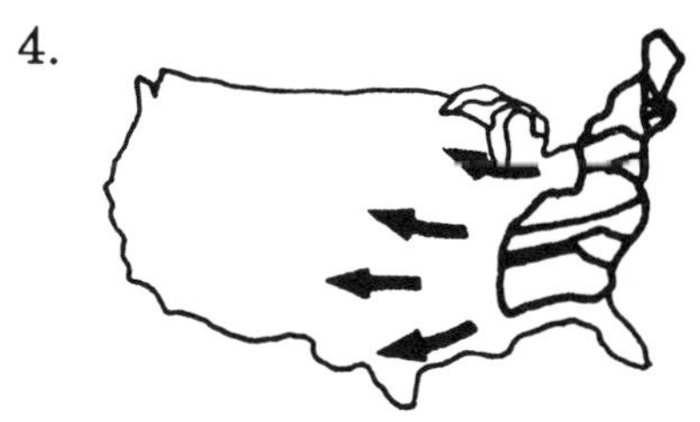 Millions of Europeans came to America as workers during the Industrial Revolution. The new nation grew and added more states. It expanded to the Pacific Ocean.

| 1840's |
| 1853 |

5.  Americans fought against one another in the Civil War between the North and the South. President Abraham Lincoln freed the slaves in the Emancipation Proclamation. The northern states won the war, and the period of Reconstruction (rebuilding) began.

| 1861 |
| 1863 |
| 1865 |

6.  The United States grew to be one of the great powers in the world. The nation fought in the First World War. After the war women got the right to vote for the first time.

    1917   1920

7.  The Great Depression began with the stock market crash. Banks, factories, and farms shut down, and many Americans were unemployed. President Franklin Roosevelt helped end the Depression with the New Deal government.

    1929   1933

8.  The United States entered the Second World War when Japan attacked the Hawaiian Islands. The war ended when the United States dropped the first atomic bombs, and the world entered the Nuclear Age.

    1941   1945

9.  Because of its distrust of and competition with the Soviet Union and other Communist nations, the United States entered a time of Cold War. Americans fought in the Korean War. The Civil Rights Movement began, and black and white Americans fought against segregation (separation of the races).

    1950's

10.  The Space Age began. Americans fought in the Vietnam War. The United States put the first men on the moon in the Apollo Program. The Women's Liberation Movement became strong. Computers began to change the nation faster than ever before.

    1960's   1970's   1980's

B   Write the dates from the box.

> 1853   1776   1955   1863   1919   1929   1492   1941   1787   1969

1. Columbus discovered North America in __*1492*__ .
2. The colonies approved the Declaration of Independence in ________.
3. The Constitution became the law of the land in ________.
4. The United States expanded to the Pacific Ocean by ________.
5. President Lincoln freed the slaves in ________.
6. The First World War ended in ________.
7. The Great Depression began in ________.
8. The United States entered the Second World War in ________.
9. The Civil Rights Movement began in ________.
10. The United States put the first men on the moon in ________.

C   Number the events in each group in time order 1-3.

1. _*2*_ The time of Reconstruction began.
   _*3*_ Banks shut down, and many Americans were unemployed.
   _*1*_ The colonies wanted to be free of British rule.

2. ___ General Washington led the colonists in the Revolutionary War.
   ___ European workers came to America during the Industrial Revolution.
   ___ George Washington became the first President of the United States.

3. ___ The northern states won the Civil War.
   ___ Americans fought in the Vietnam War.
   ___ Americans fought in the Korean War.

4. ___ Americans began to fight against segregation.
   ___ President Roosevelt established the New Deal government.
   ___ The United States entered the First World War.

D   Write T for true and F for false. Correct the false sentences.

1. ___ After Columbus discovered North America, European settlers lived in the colonies under British rule.

2. ___ England won the Revolutionary War against the American colonies.

3. ___ The Declaration of Independence became the highest law of the land.

4. ___ George Washington was the first President of the United States.

5. ___ Millions of native American Indians came to the United States as workers during the Industrial Revolution.

6. ___ Americans from the northern and southern states fought against one another during the First World War.

7. ___ President Abraham Lincoln freed the slaves with the Mayflower Compact.

8. ___ Women didn't have the right to vote in the United States until after the First World War.

9. ___ The Great Depression began with the Second World War.

10. ___ The Depression ended after Franklin Roosevelt became President and established the New Deal government.

11. ___ The United States fought against Japan in the Second World War and dropped the first atomic bombs.

12. ___ During the time of the "Cold War," the United States and the Communist Soviet Union were good friends.

13. ___ In the Civil Rights Movement Americans fought against segregation of black and white people.

14. ___ America stayed out of the Korean and the Vietnam Wars.

15. ___ In the Space Age the Women's Liberation Movement became strong.

E   Work in groups of five or more. One student makes a sentence (tells a fact) about the Exploration and Colonization period of American history. The second student repeats the first student's sentence or corrects it if necessary. He or she tells a fact about the American Revolution. The third student repeats or corrects the second student's sentence and makes a new sentence about the New Nation, and so on for all ten periods of American history.

Module 10B: Exploration and Colonization

A Exploration

1. 
In 1492 Christopher Columbus was trying to find a way from Europe to the Far East. But he didn't get to China. Instead, he found some islands in the Atlantic Ocean near North America. He thought he was near the Indies, so he called the people Indians. The Indians were native Americans. By accident, this sailor from Spain discovered a new world.

2. 
Soon other European explorers sailed across the Atlantic to learn about this exciting discovery. The Spanish explored South America in search of adventure and gold. Priests came to teach the native people.

3. 
The British and the French explored North America. Explorers traveled into the land and discovered many beautiful forests, valleys and rivers.

B Match the sentence parts. Write the letters on the lines.

1. ___ Christopher Columbus
2. ___ The Indians
3. ___ European explorers
4. ___ The Spanish
5. ___ Priests
6. ___ The British and the French

a. were native Americans

b. explored South America to find adventure and gold.

c. wanted to sail to China but discovered North America.

d. came to teach the Indians.

e. crossed the Atlantic to learn about the New World.

f. explored the land of North America.

C Colonization

1.  The Spanish established the first permanent settlement in North America. It was St. Augustine, now in the state of Florida. The British established their first permanent settlement at Jamestown, Virginia, in 1607.

2.  People from Spain, France, Holland, England, and other countries started other villages on the east coast of North America. Thirteen settlements became colonies of England. They were Virginia, Massachusetts, Maryland, Rhode Island, Connecticut, New Hampshire, North and South Carolina, New York, New Jersey, Pennsylvania, Delaware, and Georgia.

3.  Some of the native people were friendly to the colonists and taught them about the land. But other Indians attacked them. The settlers killed many Indians and took their land. They pushed the Indians to the West.

D Write T for true and F for false. Correct the false sentences.

1. ___ The British established the first permanent settlement in North America at St. Augustine, Florida.

2. ___ The first Spanish settlement was at Jamestown, Virginia, in 1607.

3. ___ Thirteen European settlements on the east coast became colonies of Spain and France.

4. ___ Some of the settlers were friendly to the native Americans and taught them about the land.

5. ___ The colonists killed many Indians and pushed them to the West.

E The Thirteen Original Colonies

Colony	Reasons for Establishment	Some Facts
1. Virginia	to find gold and to trade with Europe	The colonists wanted to be rich. They didn't want to do the difficult work to live, and many people died. Then the settlers discovered tobacco and used it for trade.
2. Massachusetts	for religious freedom	The Pilgrims came to Plymouth in 1620. The Puritans established the Massachusetts Bay Colony. They came for religious freedom, but they didn't give the same freedom to other churches.
3. Maryland	to make money from land sales	The King of England gave the land to Lord Baltimore. Lord Baltimore sold the land to settlers. He also gave religious freedom to Catholics.
4. Rhode Island	for religious freedom	Some Puritans left Massachusetts to start a new colony with religious freedom for everyone. They established the principle of separation of church and state (religion and government).
5. Connecticut	for religious freedom and economic reasons	Thomas Hooker and people from his church left Massachusetts for this new colony because the farmland was better.
6. New Hampshire	for religious, political, and economic reasons	Settlers came here from Massachusetts. They lived from fishing and trading.
7. North and South Carolina	for economic reasons	The King of England gave away the land, and the landowners rented it to settlers from Virginia and Europe.
8. New York	for political reasons	Dutch settlers were living in New Netherlands, but the British took the land from them and named it New York.

Colony	Reasons for Establishment	Some Facts
9. New Jersey	to make money from rent	Landowners rented the land to settlers.
10. Pennsylvania	for religious freedom	Willian Penn established this colony. The Quakers settled here and gave religious freedom to everyone.
11. Delaware	for political reasons	William Penn gave settlers from Pennsylvania this land because they wanted a separate government.
12. Georgia	for political and economic reasons	People came here from England because they were in debt (owed money). The government gave them land to farm.

F Make sentences about the information in E. You can use these sentence patterns.

EXAMPLE: Settlers established the colony of Virginia to find gold and to trade with Europe. Many settlers died because they didn't work enough.

Settlers established the colony of __________ | for __________.
to __________.
because ______.

G Write the letters from the map on the lines. Then tell one fact about each colony.

1. ___	Virginia		7. ___	North and South Carolina
2. ___	Massachusetts		8. ___	New York
3. ___	Maryland		9. ___	New Jersey
4. ___	Rhode Island		10. ___	Pennsylvania
5. ___	Connecticut		11. ___	Delaware
6. ___	New Hampshire		12. ___	Georgia

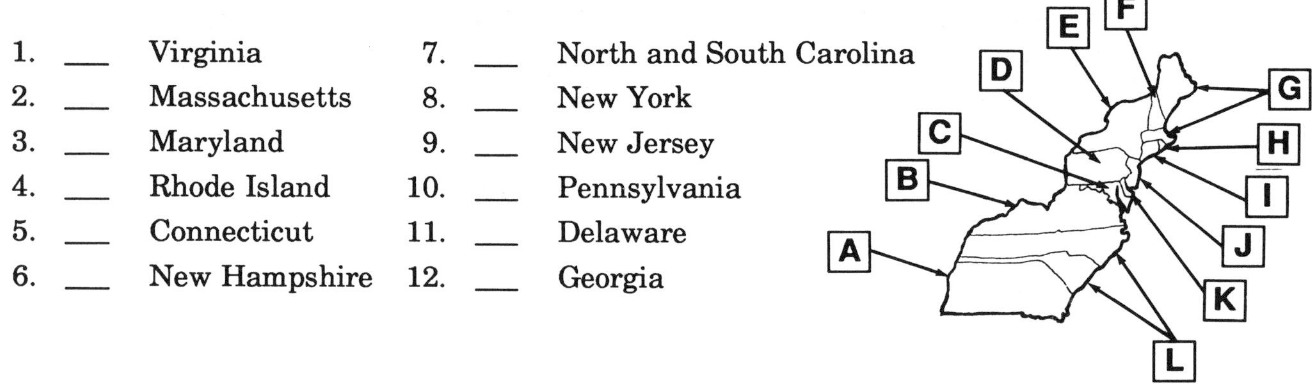

Module 10C: Revolution

A The Causes of the American Revolution

1.  The King of England allowed the thirteen American colonies a large amount of self-government. One of the reasons for this freedom was that between 1689 and 1763 England was busy with wars against France. The colonists helped the Mother Country (England) against the French in the French and Indian War.

2. 

In 1763 the war ended, and England won control over most of the colonies of North America. But by this time the colonists felt they were "Americans." They often traded with other countries. They felt strong, and they did not need the Mother Country for protection in wars anymore. They were used to freedom and self-government.

3. 

But the English needed the colonies for economic reasons. They were buying goods from the colonies at low prices and selling back manufactured products at high prices. They were also charging high taxes on American trade with other countries. Then England put new taxes on the colonists, such as the Stamp Act (taxes on printed materials).

4.  Other strict laws made life difficult for the colonists. For example, they could send their products only on British ships, and they had to sell some goods only to England at very low prices. British officials could enter homes to search for illegal goods. The colonists were not free to settle west of the Appalachian Mountains, and they had to allow British soldiers to live in their homes.

5. 

The colonists were especially angry about the "taxation without representation." They had to pay high taxes but could not send delegates to England to vote on them. In 1773 England passed the Tea Act (taxes on imported tea), so some colonists dressed up like Indians and dumped all the tea from a British ship into Boston harbor. This act was called the Boston Tea Party.

6. 

To punish the colonies and control them more closely, England passed even stricter laws. To show their unity against England, the colonies sent representatives to the First Continental Congress in Philadelphia. The Congress decided to stop buying British goods and demanded rights for the colonists in a declaration. Americans prepared for war.

B Here are some causes of the American Revolution. Write B on the lines before the sentences about the British. Write C before the sentences about the colonists.

1. ___ They were used to freedom and self-government and didn't need the Mother Country for protection anymore.

2. ___ They were buying goods at low prices and selling back manufactured products at high prices.

3. ___ Their lives were difficult because of strict laws about trade, settlement, and soldiers.

4. ___ They were angry about "taxation without representation," so they dumped tea from a ship into Boston harbor.

5. ___ To punish and have more control, they passed even stricter laws.

6. ___ To show unity, they met at the First Continental Congress and demanded their rights.

C Match the sentence parts. Write the letters on the lines.

1. ___ The American colonies had a large amount of self-government because

2. ___ England got control over North America because

3. ___ The "Boston Tea Party" occurred because

4. ___ The English passed even stricter laws because

5. ___ The colonies stopped buying British goods and prepared for war because

a. they couldn't get rights from the British.

b. they wanted to punish the colonies for the Boston Tea Party.

c. the colonists couldn't send representatives to England to vote on taxes.

d. the Mother Country was busy with wars at that time.

e. the English won the French and Indian War.

D Events of the Revolutionary War

Date	Places	Some Facts
April 19, 1775	Lexington and Concord, Massachusetts	British soldiers shot at some Minute Men (colonists ready to fight) at Lexington. The colonists fired shots at British soldiers at Concord and began the Revolutionary War.
June 1775	Boston, Massachusetts (Bunker Hill) other colonies	General George Washington led the colonists, but the colonial army did not have enough soldiers, training, or supplies. The British won many battles.
July 4, 1776	Philadelphia, Pennsylvania	Representatives of the Second Continental Congress declared the independence of the colonies from British rule. The Congress adopted the Declaration of Independence.
1778, 1779, 1780	the middle and southern colonies	The colonial army could shoot well, and George Washington gave the soldiers courage. France entered the war on the side of the colonists.
October 19, 1781	Yorktown, Virginia	The colonial army won some important battles and took control.
1783	Paris, France	The war ended. American delegates signed a peace treaty with England. America won land and independence.

 **Make sentences about the information in D. You can use these sentence patterns.**

EXAMPLES: 1. The Revolutionary War began because the British refused to give the American colonists their rights.

2. On April 19, 1775, the British shot at some Minute Men at Lexington, Massachusetts.

1. _________________________________ because _________________________________ .

2. On | _________ , _________________________ | on | _________________________ .
    In | (date) | in | (place)

F **Study the map and write words from it on the lines.**

The United States after the Treaty of Paris (1783)

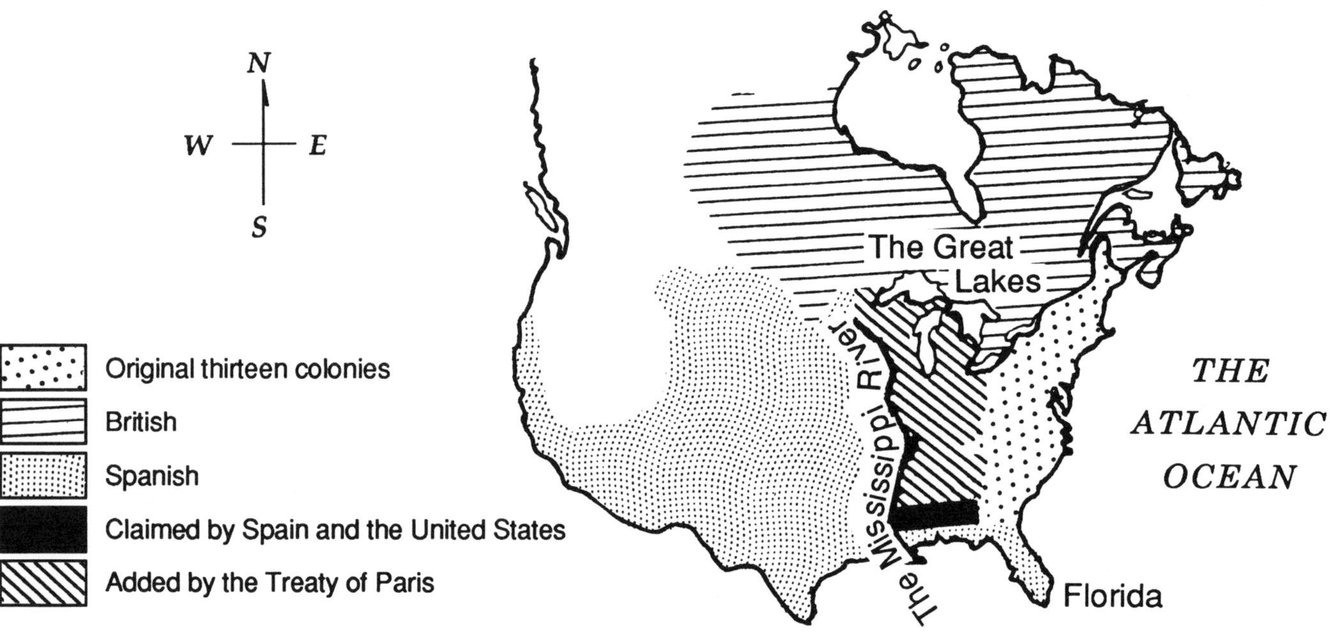

After 1783 the eastern border of the United States was (1) __the Atlantic Ocean__ , and the western border was (2) _________________________ . The (3) _________________ controlled (4) _______________ and the land west of the Mississippi River. The (5) _______________ controlled the land north of (6) _________________ .

Module 10D: Growth and Westward Movement

A From the Atlantic to the Pacific in Fifty Years

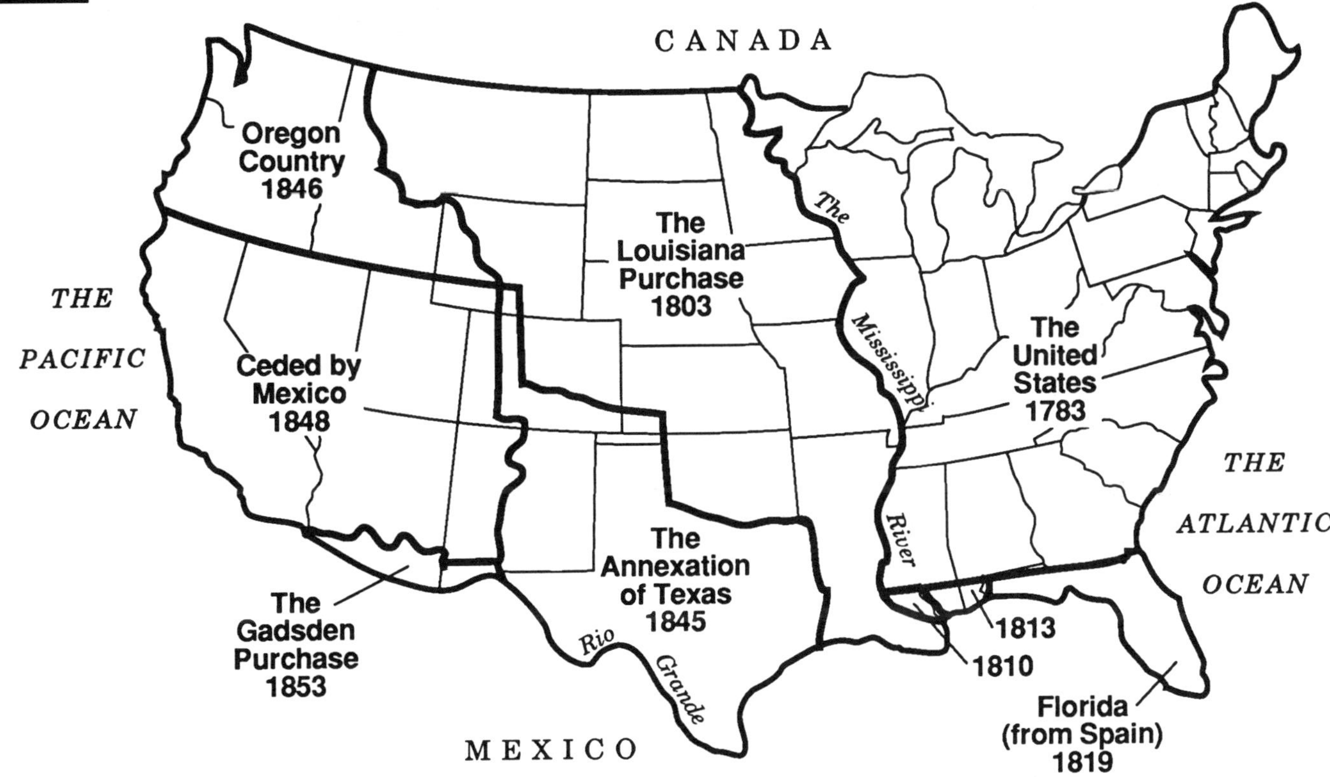

B Finish these sentences with information from the map in A.

After the American Revolution in 1783, the territory of the the United States stretched from

(1) **the Atlantic Ocean** in the East to (2) _______________ in the West. In 1803 President

Jefferson bought the territory west of the Mississippi River from France in (3) _______________.

In the year (4) ________ the U.S. obtained the land of the state of (5) _______________ from Spain.

The U.S. annexed (added) the territory of (6) _______________ in 1845. President Polk divided the

large (7) _______________ with Great Britain in 1846, and England received the northern half in

Canada. After a war in 1848, (8) _______________ ceded (had to give up) the territory from the Louisiana

Purchase to the Pacific Ocean. The U.S. paid $10 million in the year (9) ________ for some Mexican

land in the Southwest, called (10) _______________.

C   Moving West in Wagon Trains

D   Circle the correct word or words in each choice. The pictures in C suggest the answers.

Thousands of Americans moved to [1. eastern / (western)] territories to start new lives. Groups of over sixty people traveled in [2. cars / covered wagons]. Six [3. horses / oxen] pulled each wagon across the land and rivers and over hills at about [4. two / sixty] miles per hour, so a 2000-mile trip from Missouri to California took about five [5. hours / months]. No wagon traveled [6. alone / with others]. Wagon trains were important for protection against the [7. British / Indians].

At night, the wagons formed a [8. circle / long line], like a wall around a small town. The men protected the train with [9. guns / bombs]. The travelers had [10. meetings / slaves] and made rules for themselves. Everyone worked together, especially in times of danger.

E Difficult Years in Texas

Before 1836 the Texas area belonged to Spain and then to Mexico. Under the leadership of Stephen Austin, American settlers moved to Texas. The Mexican government wanted these settlers to become Mexican citizens and Roman Catholics and to free their slaves, but the settlers had other ideas. They demanded local self-government and the same rights as Americans in the United States, such as trial by jury.

The settlers declared their independence from Mexico and formed the Republic of Texas. The Mexican army of General Santa Anna defeated the rebels at the Alamo on March 6, 1836. But with the spirit of the battle cry "Remember the Alamo," Sam Houston and the Texans won a battle at San Jacinto on April 21. They signed a peace treaty with Mexican leaders and elected Houston President of the "Lone Star Republic."

The Republic of Texas did not become part of the United States for nine years because most northerners opposed the annexation of another slave state.

F Write T for true and F for false. Correct the false sentences.

1. ___ Before 1836 the area of Texas belonged to England.

2. ___ Stephen Austin was the leader of the Mexican Roman Catholics.

3. ___ The settlers in Texas believed in slavery, demanded local self-government, and wanted the rights of Americans.

4. ___ They wanted to separate from Mexico and form their own republic.

5. ___ Santa Anna was the American military leader, and Sam Houston was a Mexican general.

6. ___ The Texans had the spirit to defeat the Mexican army because they remembered the battle at the Alamo.

7. ___ The "Lone Star Republic" was the Republic of Texas.

8. ___ Jefferson Davis became the President of Texas.

9. ___ Texas became part of the U.S. right away because it was a free state.

Some Principles of the Times

In 1823 President Monroe warned European nations not to interfere with the politics of the Western Hemisphere (North and South America). The Monroe Doctrine was an example of the principle of nationalism. By the 1840's most Americans believed that the United States should expand to the Pacific Ocean because it was their "manifest destiny" (fate). The settlers organized some of the land into "territories," and these later became states. The following states were admitted officially into the Union before the time of the Civil War.

	Became a Territory	Became a State			Became a Territory	Became a State
Vermont		1791		Arkansas	1819	1836
Kentucky		1792		Michigan	1805	1837
Tennessee		1796		Florida	1822	1845
Ohio		1803		Texas		1845
Louisiana	1804	1812		Iowa	1838	1846
Indiana	1800	1816		Wisconsin	1836	1848
Mississippi	1798	1817		California		1850
Illinois	1809	1818		Minesota	1849	1858
Alabama	1817	1819		Oregon	1848	1859
Maine		1820		Kansas	1854	1861
Missouri	1812	1821				

Correct these false sentences.

1. In the Monroe Doctrine, President Madison warned ~~South American~~ European nations not to interfere with the politics of Europe.

2. The doctrine was an example of the principle of separatism.

3. Because of the principle of "taxation without representation," many Americans thought that the U.S. should expand to the Mississippi River.

4. Some of the land became "countries," and these were later admitted into the House of Representatives as states.

Make sentences about the information in G. You can use these sentence patterns.

1. ____________ | was organized as a territory | in ________ .
    (state) | was admitted as a state | (year)

2. ________ became a | territory | before | ________ .
    (state) | state | in the same year as | (state)

Module 10E: The Time of the Civil War

A   The Causes of the Civil War

In the 1800s the northern and the southern states disagreed on basic issues. Their differences led to the Civil War.

The North...

...lived from industry and the manufacture of goods such as clothing and furniture. Northern factories did not use slaves. The abolitionists (opponents of slavery) worked to free the slaves.

...produced expensive products and got the U.S. government to put a protectionist tax on products from other countries.

...was adding free states to the Union and had a larger population than the South. The northern states had more representatives in Congress than the southern ones.

...believed in the unity of the United States and opposed the separation of the southern states from the Union.

...supported the election of Abraham Lincoln as President of the United States.

The South...

...depended on agriculture for its economy. The main crop was cotton, and southern planters felt they needed slave workers to make money. They opposed the abolition of slavery.

...preferred cheap European goods to the expensive products of northern factories and opposed the protective tax on them.

...was adding slave states to the Union but had a smaller population than the North. The southern states were losing power in the House of Representatives.

...opposed federal laws and seceded (separated) from the Union by creating the Confederate States of America.

...opposed the election of Lincoln and chose Jefferson Davis President of the Confederacy.

B   Make sentences about the information in A. You can use these sentence patterns and the pictures on the next page for ideas.

1. The northern states ______________________________, but the southern states
    ______________________________.

2. Although the North ______________________________, the South ______________________________.

3. The states of the North ______________________________. On the other hand, the states of the South ______________________________.

1.

2.

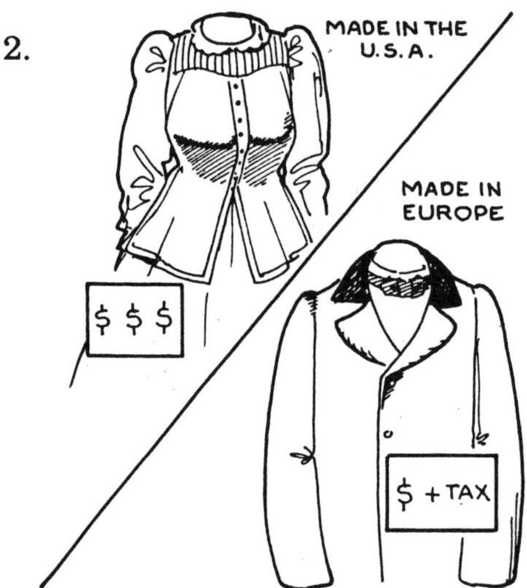

3.

4.

C Finish each sentence about the map on the next page with the names of different states.

EXAMPLE: During the time of the Civil War, the state of Illinois was free, but Tennessee was a slave state.

1. During the time of the Civil War, the state of ___________ was free, but ___________ was a slave state.

2. The state of ___________ seceded from the Union to become part of the Confederacy (the Confederate States of America).

3. Although ___________ was a slave state, it did not secede.

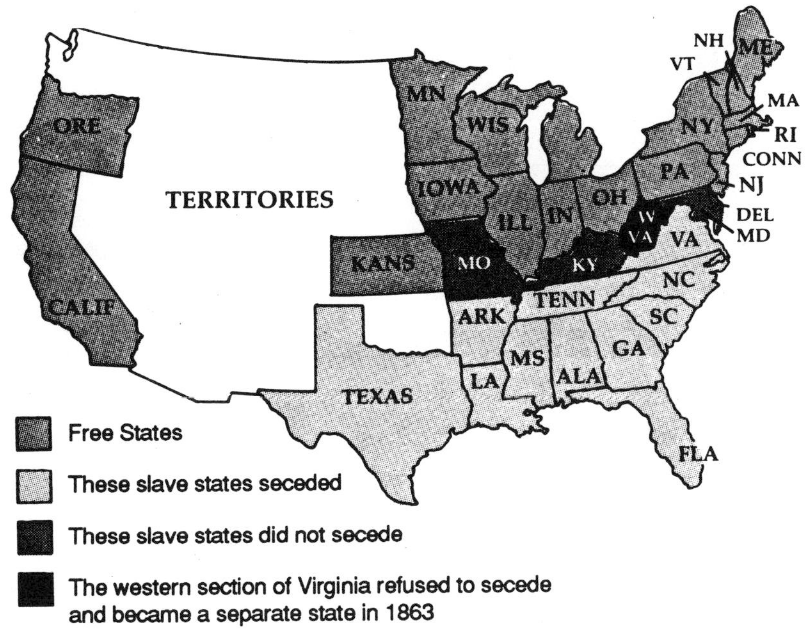

D   The Strengths of Both Sides in the Civil War

The War Between the States divided not only the country but also families. It was long and difficult because each side had advantages, so the North and the South were about equal in strength.

Both sides had excellent generals: Ulysses S. Grant for the Union and Robert E. Lee for the Confederacy. The North was richer, and its factories supplied its army with weapons. Most of the railroads were in the North, and the Union controlled the U.S. Navy. Supplies for the Confederate army, on the other hand, had to travel only short distances. Its soldiers had more spirit because they were fighting for their own land.

E   Write N on the line before each sentence about the North. Write S before each sentence about the South.

1. __N__   General Ulysses S. Grant was the military leader.

2. ___   General Robert E. Lee led the army.

3. ___   It got weapons for its army from its own factories.

4. ___   It controlled most of the railroads and the U.S. Navy.

5. ___   Its army got supplies more quickly because they didn't have to travel long distances.

6. ___   Its army was defending its own land, so the soldiers had more spirit.

F   Events of the Civil War

Date	Place	Some Facts
July 1861	Bull Run (near Washington D.C.)	Spectators from Washington came to watch the battle as entertainment. To their surprise, the Confederate army defeated Union forces.
1861 1862	The East The West	Neither side was winning. Then General Grant won many battles and demanded the surrender of the Confederates.
January 1, 1863		In the Emancipation Proclamation, President Abraham Lincoln announced that the slaves in all states under Confederate control were free. The proclamation weakened the spirit of the South.
July 1863	Gettysburg, Pennsylvania	The North won an important battle. Lincoln made a famous speech, the Gettysburg Address, at the battlefield.
1863 1864	Georgia and the Carolinas	The army of General William Sherman marched through the South and destroyed homes, plantations, and railroads. The cruelty of the soldiers destroyed the spirit of the South.
April 3, 1865	Richmond, Virginia	The North captured the Confederate capital. General Lee surrendered at Appomattox Court House. The war was over.

G   Work in pairs or groups. Make sentences about the information in F. You can use this sentence pattern. Your classmates will answer "true" or "false."

EXAMPLES: Student 1:   In July 1861, spectators from Washington, D.C. came to watch a battle at Bull Run.

Student 2:   True. On this day the Union forces defeated the Confederate army as expected.

Student 1:   False. The Confederate forces defeated the Union army, and everyone was surprised.

On | ________, | _______________ | in | ___________.
In | (date) | | at | (place)

Module 10F: Industrialization

A **Work in pairs. Look only at this page and ask your partner these questions about the time of Reconstruction. Your partner will tell you the answers from the information on the next page. Write them on the lines.**

1. When was the period of Reconstruction? _____ *from 1865 to 1877* _______

2. How did Republicans of the North help ex-slaves during this time? _______
    ____

3. What did the 13th Amendment to the U.S. Constitution do? _______________
    ____

4. What were the 14th and 15th Amendments? _______________________________

5. How did the North punish the South? ___________________________________

6. What couldn't former southern leaders do? ______________________________

7. Why didn't white southerners accept the new laws? ______________________
    ____

8. What happened to the U.S. during the time of Reconstruction? ___________
    ____

B **To answer your partner's questions, find the information and tell it to your partner. He or she will write the answers.**

The Industrial Revolution

Before the nineteenth century, people produced most goods by hand. But during the Industrial Revolution, machines changed the methods of production, and America grew to be an industrial power. Mass production made manufacturing quick and cheap.

Many important inventions of the Industrial Revolution were the work of Americans. Some examples are Eli Whitney's cotton gin and Elias Howe's sewing machine. Alexander Graham Bell invented the telephone, and Thomas A. Edison invented the phonograph and the electric light bulb. Farmers produced more food with machines. Many people left the farms to work in factories in big cities, and these cities became large markets for factory-made products. The federal government helped industry. It passed high tariffs (taxes) to keep out foreign products and supported the free exchange of goods among the states.

 **Work in pairs. Look only at this page. To answer your partner's questions, find the information and tell it to your partner. He or she will write the answers.**

The Time of Reconstruction

The period of Reconstruction was from 1865 to 1877. During this time, Republicans of the North helped ex-slaves with housing, education, and food. Congress passed three Amendments to the U.S. Constitution:

- Amendment 13 put an end to slavery.
- Amendment 14 made all blacks citizens.
- Amendment 15 gave blacks the right to vote.

The North also wanted to punish the South, so Congress established military government in the southern states. Former southern leaders could not hold political office. Few white southerners believed that blacks were equal to whites, so they opposed the new laws. But black people had some political power in the South.

Although the differences between the North and the South were great, the United States became one nation again.

 **Now ask your partner these questions about the Industrial Revolution. Your partner will tell you the answers from the information on the previous page. Write them on the lines.**

1. What happened during the Industrial Revolution? _______________________________________

   ____

2. What did Eli Whitney invent? ____

3. What was Elias Howe's invention? ____

4. Who invented the telephone? ____

5. Who invented the phonograph and the light bulb? _____________________________________

6. Why did many people leave the farms? ____

7. What were the markets for factory-made products? ____________________________________

8. How did the federal government help industry? ____

   ____

C The Labor Movement

Since the Industrial Revolution, labor unions have fought for safe and healthy working conditions, fair wages, an eight-hour workday, job security, health benefits, pension plans, workers' rights, and civil rights.

Beginning Date	Union	Founder	Activities
1869	the Knights of Labor	Uriah S. Stephens	This union represented all workers, but it wasn't very successful.
1881	the American Federation of Labor (AFL)	Samuel Gompers	This union represented only skilled workers. It got them higher wages, shorter hours, and better working conditions.
1938	the Congress of Industrial Organizations (CIO)	John L. Lewis	This union represented semi-skilled and skilled workers. Its strikes shut down whole industries, not just individual factories.
1955	AFL-CIO	(merger)	The AFL joined the CIO and was powerful until President Reagan's government weakened the unions.

D Write the name of the union before each sentence: the Knights of Labor, the AFL, the CIO, or the AFL-CIO.

1. _CIO_ This union began with John L. Lewis.
2. ______ Uriah S. Stephens founded (established) this union.
3. ______ Samuel Gompers was the founder.
4. ______ This early union wasn't very successful.
5. ______ This union represented semi-skilled workers, and its strikes shut down whole industries.
6. ______ This union got higher wages, shorter hours, and better working conditions for skilled workers.
7. ______ This union was a merger of two big unions.
8. ______ President Reagan's government reduced the power of this union.

 **A Political Party and a Movement**

Farmers formed the Populist Party in 1892. They felt that big business had too much power and that the system was unfair to farmers and industrial workers. They also believed in government control of the railroads and the telephone system. They wanted a graduated income tax (a higher percentage of tax on higher incomes), secret ballots (voting), and direct election of U.S. Senators by the people, not by state legislatures. Populists became mayors of towns, state representatives, and even Senators. They lost power after the election of 1896, but their ideas influenced the major political parties.

In the first part of the twentieth century, progressive thinkers formed a movement for social reform. Progressives believed in a "square deal" for ordinary Americans, so they tried to help workers, small businesses, and farmers. They wanted the federal government to control big business, take responsibility for the quality of food and drugs, and protect the environment. Some leaders of the Progressive Movement held political office and made reforms. Their ideas also led to several amendments to the Constitution: the Sixteenth Amendment established the federal income tax, and the Seventeenth Amendment allowed voters to elect U.S. Senators directly.

 **Answer these questions about the political party and the movement.**

	The Populist Party	The Progressive Movement
1. Who formed it?		
2. When?		
3. What did the members believe?		
4. What did they want?		
5. What did they do?		

Module 10G: The U.S. Becomes a World Power

Work in pairs. Look only at this page and ask your partner these questions about World War I. Your partner will tell you the answers from the next page. Take notes on the information.

1. What happened to begin World War I?   *Heir to the throne of Austria-Hungary was shot. Austria-Hungary declared war on Serbia.*

2. What were the two sides in the war, and what European countries joined them?

3. Why did the United States enter the war in 1917?

4. Why was World War I called "the Great War"?

5. How and when did the war end?

6. What was the basis of the peace treaty to end the war?

7. What was the League of Nations, and why did it fail?

B   The Great Depression

Because American goods were too expensive for other countries to buy and American wages were low, many investors lost confidence in the stock market and sold their stocks (shares, or part ownership, of companies). The Great Depression began with the stock market crash on Black Tuesday, October 29, 1929. Thousands of businesses, factories, and banks closed down, and millions of workers lost their jobs. This time of economic depression lasted for ten years.

President Franklin D. Roosevelt helped end the Great Depression with his "New Deal" of relief, recovery, and reform ("the Three R's"). His government relieved suffering with payments to unemployed people and loans to farmers and homeowners. It created government jobs to help the economy recover. Roosevelt also worked on economic reform to prevent future depressions.

A　**Work in pairs. Look only at this page. To answer your partner's questions about World War I, find the information and tell it to your partner. He or she will take notes.**

- It was Woodrow Wilson's plan for a world organization to prevent future wars. To avoid involvement in world affairs, the U.S. Senate rejected the Treaty of Versailles and the plan for the League of Nations.

- It was a "total war" because it involved the economies and the people of many countries. The U.S. Congress passed the Selective Service Acts to draft young men into the armed forces.

- The basis of the Treaty of Versailles was President Wilson's plan for peace, his Fourteen Points. Among other things, Wilson wanted freedom of the seas and trade and self-determination (the right of people to decide on their own form of government).

- Austria-Hungary declared war on the small country of Serbia because an assassin shot the heir to their throne.

- Americans were angry because Germany was using submarines to attack both warships and trade ships. They wanted to fight this "war to end all wars."

- The Central Powers were Austria-Hungary and Germany, and the Allied Powers were Russia, France, England, and Italy.

- Germany signed an armistice on November 11, 1918.

C　**Match the sentence parts. Write the letters on the lines.**

1. _d_ Many people lost confidence in the U.S. economy because...

2. ___ The Great Depression began because...

3. ___ Millions of workers lost their jobs because...

4. ___ The Depression ended ten years later because...

5. ___ The government made payments to the unemployed, farmers, and homeowners because...

6. ___ The New Deal government created jobs because...

a. businesses, factories, and banks closed.

b. Roosevelt wanted to relieve economic suffering.

c. investors sold their stocks, and the stock market crashed.

d. American goods were expensive, but wages were low.

e. President Roosevelt started the New Deal of relief, recovery, and reform.

f. it wanted the U.S. to recover from the Depression and prevent future ones.

 **Work in pairs. Look only at this page and ask your partner these questions about World War II. You partner will tell you the answers from the next page. Take notes on the information.**

1. What happened to begin World War II?   *Germany invaded Poland.*
   Germany, Italy, Japan – the Axis. France, England, the Soviet Union – the Allies.

2. Why did the United States stay out of the war at first?

3. Why did the U.S. finally enter the war?

4. What happened during the war in Europe?

5. How and when did World War II end?

6. What were the effects of the war?

E Organizations and Plans

After World War II, the Allied countries organized the United Nations (the U.N.) to solve problems among nations and keep the peace. Although this world organization had many of the same principles as the League of Nations, this time the United States was one of its original members. But at the same time the U.S. and the Soviet Union (the U.S.S.R.) were beginning to compete for power.

In 1947 under the Truman Doctrine, the U.S. government gave $400 million in economic and military aid to keep Greece and Turkey free of Soviet control. Then the U.S. established the Marshall Plan to rebuild the countries of Western Europe, including its former enemies.

The period of history after World War II is known as the Cold War because the U.S. and the U.S.S.R., with their opposing economic and political systems, have been trying to win influence and control over other countries through economic aid rather than weapons. In 1949 the U.S. and the nations of Western Europe formally allied in the North Atlantic Treaty Organization (NATO) to defend one another against attack. The U.S.S.R. began the Warsaw Pact with Eastern Europe in 1955.

 **Work in pairs. Look only at this page. To answer your partner's questions about World War II, find the information and tell it to your partner. He or she will take notes.**

- President Truman made the decision to drop the atomic bomb on Hiroshima and Nagasaki. Japan surrendered on August 10, 1945.

- Germany invaded countries and enslaved, tortured, and killed many groups of people. The Soviet Union pushed back the attack of the German army. Italy surrendered in 1943. On "D-Day" in 1944, the U.S. General Dwight D. Eisenhower led the Allied armies to victory in Europe. In May 1945, Germany surrendered unconditionally.

- Congress wanted to avoid involvement in world affairs and stay neutral. In the 1930s it passed Neutrality Acts to keep the seas free.

- The army of Adolf Hitler invaded Poland. The other Axis countries (Italy and Japan) supported Germany, and the Allies (France, England and later the Soviet Union) opposed Germany.

- Over 22 million people died. The U.S. and the U.S.S.R. became the two leading powers in the world.

- Japan attacked Pearl Harbor in Hawaii, so the U.S. declared war on Japan, and Germany and Italy declared war on the U.S.

F **Write T for true and F for false. Correct the false sentences.**

1. ___ The purpose of the United Nations is to solve world problems and prevent war.

2. ___ The U.S. Congress rejected the plan for the United Nations because it wanted to avoid involvement and stay neutral.

3. ___ After World War II, the U.S. and the countries of Western Europe began to compete for world political power.

4. ___ The Truman Doctrine is an example of the U.S. attempt to influence other countries through economic and military aid.

5. ___ Under the Marshall Plan, China gave aid to rebuild Japan.

6. ___ In general, the U.S. and its allies have a different political and economic system from that of the U.S.S.R. and its allies.

7. ___ During the Cold War, the nations of Western Europe have allied with the U.S.S.R. in NATO, and the U.S. has allied with Eastern Europe in the Warsaw Pact.

Module 10H: Modern Times

A **Work in groups of four. Each of you studies the information about a different aspect of modern times. In turn, summarize your information in your own words for the group.**

1. After World War II, America went to war twice against communist countries and their supporters. In 1950, North and South Korea could not agree on a common form of govermnent. North Korean communists, supported by the Chinese, invaded South Korea. The United Nations supported South Korea, and the United States sent troops (soldiers). With U.S. help, the South Koreans pushed the communist troops back to the thirty-eighth parallel.

Before the Vietnamese war, Vietnam was a colony of France. The people didn't want war, but they wanted freedom from foreign powers. Between 1961 and 1975, the United States intervened in the conflict on the side of the South Vietnamese anticommunists. The desire for independence gave the Vietnamese their fighting spirit. There were many protests against the war, and the United States finally withdrew.

2. The period of history since the invention of atomic bomb at the end of World War II is the Age of Technology and the Atomic Age. The world powers and people of all nations know that a nuclear war could destroy the whole planet. However, the superpowers, mainly the United States and the Soviet Union, continue to build missiles, bombs, military aircraft, and space weapons.

Fortunately, not all technology is designed for war. The United States sent its first satellite into space in 1958, and by 1969, the first American stepped onto the moon. Since then, the whole world has been using satellites and other space technology for communication, weather forecasting, science, and business. Both U.S. and Soviet shuttles are building space stations for both peaceful and military purposes.

At the heart of the Age of Technology is the computer. To school children, the computer is as important as the pencil. In the future, it can be used to improve human lives and to solve many of the world's serious problems, such as hunger and poverty.

3. In the 1950s, "the American dream" of wealth and freedom was easier for white males to achieve than for members of minority groups. Black Americans in the South, for example, could not attend white schools or live in white neighborhoods. Because of the policy of segregation, blacks sat in the backs of buses, used only restrooms for nonwhites, and ate at nonwhite lunch counters. In some southern states, black people could not even vote. Northerners, too, often discriminated against blacks, especially in jobs and housing.

In 1957, President Dwight D. Eisenhower sent U.S. troops to Little Rock, Arkansas, to force the all-white university there to accept black students. Between 1957 and 1970, as a result of the civil rights movement led by Martin Luther King, Jr., new laws helped blacks and other minorities to achieve equality. Presidents John F. Kennedy and Lyndon B. Johnson used King's ideas in their New Frontier and Great Society programs.

There have been great changes in the last forty years, but nonwhites have not yet achieved equal status today.

4. For a long time, American men did not believe in equality of the sexes. Women worked in low-level jobs and usually received lower pay than men for equal work. Few women finished college, and even fewer rose to executive-level positions with high salaries.

Today, American women are still fighting for equality because their salaries are generally lower than men's. However, many changes in the positions of the sexes have occurred. Half of all college students are women. More women are working than ever before, and their pay has risen, especially in government jobs, because it is easier for women to get jobs that used to be for men only. Many women own businesses, and others are executives in private business and government.

In recent years, many citizens have tried to add an amendment to the U.S. Constitution. The "Equal Rights Amendment" (ERA) states that both sexes have equal rights. But because many people fear that the amendment could take away some of women's special protections, such as the right to alimony (financial support after divorce) and exemption from the military draft, the amendment was not ratified (approved by enough states).

B   Match the sentence parts. Write the letters on the lines.

1. _d_ North Korean and Chinese communists invaded South Korea because

2. ___ The United States finally withdrew from the Vietnam conflict because

3. ___ The United States and the Soviet Union continue to build missiles, bombs, and space weapons even though

4. ___ The whole world has been using space technology for communication, weather forecasting, and science since

5. ___ In the 1950s, black Americans could not attend white schools or live in white neighborhoods because

6. ___ Especially in jobs and salaries, nonwhites and women are still not equal to white males today even though

7. ___ Many American women are still fighting for equality today because

8. ___ The Equal Rights Amendment was not ratified because

a. great changes have occurred in the last forty years.

b. southern states followed a policy of segregation.

c. a nuclear war would destroy the whole planet.

d. the country could not agree on a common form of government.

e. many people oppose the loss of special protections for women.

f. women's salaries are generally lower than men's for equal work.

g. the people fought hard for the independence of their country from foreign powers.

h. the United States sent its first satellite into space in 1958.

C   Correct these false sentences.

1. After World War II, America went to war twice against capitalist countries and their supporters.

2. In the Korean War, North Koreans pushed Chinese troops back to the thirty-eighth parallel with help from the United States.

3. The Age of Technology began around the time of the discovery of the moon.

4. In 1957, President Eisenhower sent U.S. troops to Vietnam to oppose the followers of Martin Luther King, Jr. in the civil rights movement.

5. The New Frontier and Great Society programs were plans for U.S. and Soviet shuttle space stations.

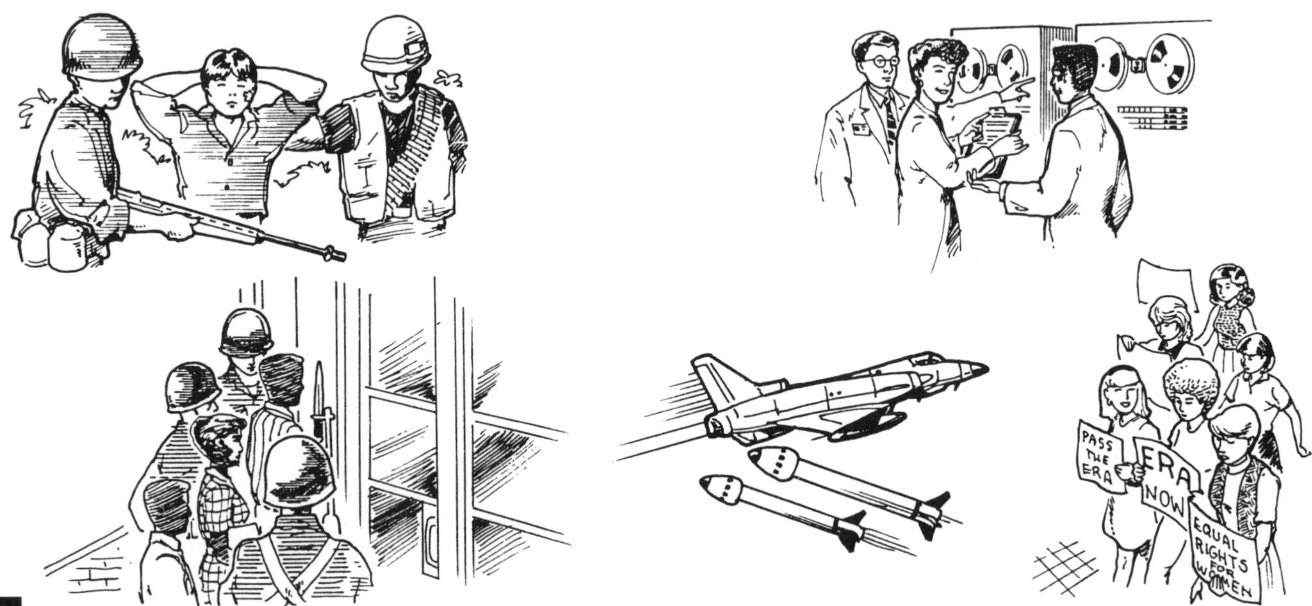

D   **Do you support or oppose these statements about modern U.S. history? Work in small groups. Each student in turn chooses a different topic and speaks about it for one or two minutes. The other students tell their opinions and discuss the issue. Then summarize your discussion for the class.**

1.   The United States should send troops to other countries if the conflict involves communism.

2.   All nations have the right to be independent from foreign powers and to determine their own form of government.

3.   The superpowers must continue to build missiles, bombs, military aircraft, and space weapons.

4.   Because space weapons would destroy the earth, the United States and the Soviet Union should stop the development of space technology.

5.   Because of the computer, humanity will solve many of the world's important problems, such as hunger and poverty.

6.   Members of minority groups have not been able to achieve "the American dream" or equal status with whites because of the policies of segregation and discrimination.

7.   The U.S. government has the responsibility of forcing the states to carry out civil rights laws and policies.

8.   Men should do "men's work" and women should do "women's work" because the sexes are different.

9.   Because there is no discrimination in job status and salary today, there is no need to fight for "equal pay for equal work."

10.   The "Equal Rights Amendment" (ERA) is a necessary addition to the U.S. Constitution.

E   **Make a statement of your own about modern U.S. history. Speak about it to the class for one or two minutes. The other students tell their opinions and discuss the issue.**